KITCHEN COLLECTIBLES

AN ILLUSTRATED
PRICE GUIDE

KITCHEN
COLLECTIBLES

AN ILLUSTRATED PRICE GUIDE

ELLEN M. PLANTE
Photos by Ted Plante

Wallace-Homestead Book Company
Radnor, Pennsylvania

Copyright © 1991 by Ellen M. Plante

All Rights Reserved

Published in Radnor, Pennsylvania 19089, by Wallace-Homestead,
a division of Chilton Book Company

Designed by Anthony Jacobson
Manufactured in the United States of America.

Library of Congress Cataloging in Publication Data

Plante, Ellen M.
    Kitchen collectibles : an illustrated price guide / Ellen M.
  Plante ; photos by Ted Plante.
      p. cm.
    Includes bibliographical references and index.
    ISBN 0-87069-609-2—ISBN 0-87069-581-9 (pbk.)
    1. Kitchen utensils—United States—History.   2. Kitchen utensils—
  United States—Collectibles.   I. Title.
  TX656.P58   1991   91-2104
  683'.82—dc20   CIP

2 3 4 5 6 7 8 9 0   0 9 8 7 6 5 4 3 2

For Kelly and Christopher

Contents

Preface

In April 1919 the *Ladies' Home Journal* published an article written by Olga Samaroff, the foremost female pianist in the United States during the early 1900s. Her article, entitled "My Experiences in My Kitchen," told readers about one cold winter evening when Olga sat in her kitchen waiting for the cook to return from an errand. As she waited she surveyed her cozy, spotless kitchen, and of it she wrote, "Here, from all ends of the earth are gathered the elements which give us life and strength and health. These elements are prepared in ways which represent an immense amount of scientific research. They also represent the development of great industries, the backbone of national prosperity. . . . There is no end to the appeal to the imagination when one begins to think about the contents of a kitchen in that light."

These words, written so many years ago, capture the essence of collecting old kitchenware today. We are reminded of the centuries of human ingenuity and creativity that have propelled us forward so we may look back with respect and appreciation for the tools of the Victorian era. We are encouraged to remember the young sciences and industries that have given us conveniences, and not just necessities.

Today we find that the kitchen, often combined with the eating area and family room, has come full circle. Like the rural country kitchen of a century ago, today's kitchen is a multifunctional space often considered the heart of the home. As a result there is a steadily growing interest in old kitchenware as collectors, decorators, and admirers seek out the multitude of kitchen-related items that bring a piece of history, a touch of nostalgia, and an age-old warmth to the kitchen of the 1990s.

Readers will note that all photo captions include the asking price of the object pictured, which is not always the same as the selling price. Collectors must keep in mind that supply and demand, the region of the county in which an object is located, and ultimately, what collectors are willing to pay for a piece, will all have a significant impact on pricing. Most photographs were taken at large antiques shows with dealer representation from across the country.

To all who turn the pages of this book, welcome to the world of kitchen antiques and collectibles, a diverse area that is constantly expanding to include new treasures.

Acknowledgments

It is with sincere appreciation and gratitude that I thank the following family members, friends, collectors, dealers, manufacturers, historical societies, libraries, and all others that contributed to the reality of this book on kitchen collectibles.

To my husband, Ted, thank you for your unending support and fine photographic efforts—this is as much your book as mine.

To all those friends, collectors, and dealers who allowed us to photograph their special kitchenware items, thank you for your interest and support. Thanks go to Jack and Bonita Baldwin, Norwalk, Ohio; The Bear and Unusual, Saugerties, New York; The Blue Cat Antiques and Collectibles, Woodstock, Connecticut; Blue House Antiques, Lewisburg, Pennsylvania; Karol Boyd, Lewiston, New York; Brownstead Antiques, Whitney Point, New York; Chestnut Ridge Antiques, Groton, New York; The Closetful, Clinton, New York; Marge Conibear, Lewiston, New York; Donna Conyer, Pittsford, New York; Country Kitchen Antiques, Huntington, New York; Country Lady Antiques, Saratoga Springs, New York; Gene and Joan Currier, Currier Antiques, Snyder, New York; Dad's Follies, Winchester, Massachusetts; Foundation Antiques, Fair Haven, Vermont; Susan Gmyrek, Buffalo, New York; Rita and "Red" Hare, Treasures of Old, Boca Raton, Florida; Ann and Fred Heuer, Lewiston, New York; Faith Johns, Poughkeepsie, New York; Babe Kinnemeyer, Cincinnati, Ohio; Lorrie Kitchen and Dan Tucker, Toledo, Ohio; Richard Lobene, Rochester, New York; Neil McCurdy, Coopersburg, Pennsylvania; McFarland Enterprises, Elma, New York; Roger Metzger, Roger's Antiques and Collectables, Williamsville, New York; Karen Nevins, Reading, Pennsylvania; Olde Town Road Antiques, Upton, Massachusetts; Past Time Antiques, Lewiston, New York; Pembroke Peddler, Bryantville,

Massachusetts; Mimi Pyne, Lewiston, New York; Angela F. Riley, Lockport, New York; Fran and Betty Rooney, Youngstown, New York; Running Deer Antiques, Lewiston, New York; Donna Segarra, Youngstown, New York; Spring House Antiques, Oakwood, Illinois; Nettie and Clark Stimpson, The Country Barn, Wilson, New York; T & J's Yesteryear Collectables, Canton, Connecticut; Irene M. Tarquino, Orchard Park, New York; Shirley and Gregory Urtel, Lockport, New York; Natalie Warner, 1843 House, Stafford Springs, Connecticut; and Mr. and Mrs. John Weatherbee of Blue Goose Antiques in Hampden, Maine, for old advertisements they located and sent to me.

A special thank-you goes to noted expert and dealer Bob Cahn, "The Primitive Man," of Carmel, New York, for his valuable time, interest and the wide assortment of "unusuals" he made available for photographing at the Madison-Bouckville Show in August 1990.

A special thank-you to David T. Pikul of the Chuctanunda Antique Company of Amsterdam, New York, for offering his valuable time during the Antique Expo in Clarence, New York. He pointed out rare and unusual examples of his beautiful French enameled ware and other kitchenware items we photographed.

Regarding photographs, thank you to Mr. James Shannahan, JBS Photo Service in North Tonawanda, New York. Without Mr. Shannahan's professional advice and expert skill in developing and making our photos "reproduction ready," we would have been lost.

For letters answered and for the volumes of information sent in response to my requests, I'd like to thank General Electric Company and especially Franklin Friday of Friday Associates, Inc., of Louisville, Kentucky. Friday is the author and editor of *A Walk Through the Park*, a book that presents the history of GE's development and Appliance Park. Mr. Friday provided background material as well as copies of photos and offers of additional assistance.

Thank you to Proctor-Silex, Inc. and Beth Harris McMahon, Marketing Communications Associate, in Glen Allen, Virginia, for copies from trade catalogs and a listing of additional resource materials and contacts.

Thank you to KitchenAid, Inc. and especially Don Stuart, manager of marketing communications in St. Joseph, Michigan, for information pertaining to the history of the company; to Toastmaster Inc., and Tina Ferling, sales promotion administrator in Columbia, Missouri; General Mills, Inc. and Jean Toll, corporate archivist in Minneapolis, Minnesota; Hobart Corporation and Pat Warner, graphics specialist of PMI Food Equipment in Troy, Ohio; and United States Stove Company, Chattanooga, Tennessee, for information sent.

A thank-you goes to the following for their time and consideration in helping me locate pertinent information about kitchen furniture: Barbara Armstrong, executive director of the Elwood, Indiana, Chamber of Commerce, who provided me with information on Sellers Kitchen Cabinets; Mrs. Evelyn S. Clift, curator of the Henry County Historical Society, Inc. of New Castle, Indiana, for information on the Hoosier Manufacturing Company; and the Lebanon Public Library in Lebanon, Indiana, for information on Boone kitchen cabinets.

Thank you to William W. Jenny, regional historic site administrator, Plymouth Notch Historic District, Plymouth, Vermont, for the photograph of the Calvin Coolidge Homestead kitchen and descriptive information.

Finally, thank you to all the people at Wallace-Homestead Book Company and especially Tim Scott, manuscript editor, and Harry Rinker, editorial consultant, for giving me the opportunity to see this project through and for all their valuable advice and recommendations.

Introduction

 Our knowledge of kitchen collectibles can be enhanced greatly by understanding the evolution of the kitchen during the nineteenth and early twentieth centuries. During the period from 1800 to the 1850s, the kitchen was a part of the multipurpose "keeping room" that served as the center of family activity. The all-important fireplace was used to prepare meals, warm the room, and serve as an additional light source.

Necessary kitchen tools included iron pots, a Dutch oven, trivets of various sizes, skillets, and a long-handled toaster.

Woodenware, redware pottery, and stoneware were the utilitarian vessels used to store, prepare, and serve foods.

In warmer climates and in growing towns and cities, the kitchen often was located in a separate cookhouse or in the back of the home.

Kitchens changed very little until the mid-nineteenth century, when the cookstove was introduced. By this time many middle-class families employed domestic help, and as the house grew in size the kitchen expanded to include multiple workrooms where specific household chores were performed.

In 1861 the complete works of Mrs. Isabella Beeton were published in a book entitled *Beeton's Book of Household Management*. On the subject of "Arrangement and Economy of the Kitchen," Mrs. Beeton wrote, "it must be remembered that it [the kitchen] is the great laboratory of every household, and that much of the 'weal or woe' as far as regards bodily health, depends upon the nature of the preparations concocted within its walls."

Mrs. Beeton suggested that the construction of a kitchen should include good lighting and ventilation and access without passing through the main house. She also advised her readers that the kitchen should be far enough removed from the rest of the house so that family and guests would not be offended by cooking odors and noises (one reason why many mid to

The late nineteenth-century kitchen at the Calvin Coolidge Homestead, Plymouth Notch, Vt. Courtesy Vermont Division for Historic Preservation.

late nineteenth-century kitchens were in the basement or located at the rear of the house). Finally, Mrs. Beeton recommended the scullery, pantry, and storeroom should be close to the kitchen to save steps.

The kitchen of the 1860s contained a small cast-iron cookstove, table, freestanding cupboard, and zinc-lined sink. There were probably sadirons and a copper teakettle warming atop the stove, a towel rack and shelf full of necessities hanging on a wall, and a grandfather clock in the corner.

The food pantry, or storeroom, housed the staples on rows of shelving or in stoneware crocks, and the scullery provided a place for cleaning and preparing foodstuffs for cooking.

A laundry room for the tedious task of washing and ironing also might have been located close to the kitchen.

Regarding kitchen tools, utensils, and dishware, Isabella Beeton suggested that "amongst the most essential requirements of the kitchen are scales or weighing machines for family use . . . accompanying the scales, or weighing machines, there should be spice-boxes, and sugar and biscuit canisters of either white or japanned tin . . . copper boilers, saucepans, soup pots, kettles . . . stone and earthenware vessels and common dishes."

Another popular nineteenth-century household guide was the 1869 *American Woman's Home* by Catherine Beecher and Harriet Beecher Stowe. Full of new and innovative concepts regarding the kitchen,

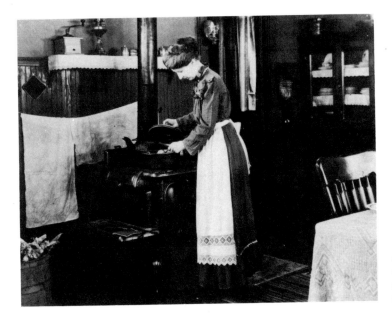

A turn-of-the-century kitchen complete with cast-iron cookstove. Courtesy of GE Appliance Historical Archives.

this book about the principles of domestic science advised "if parents wish their daughters to grow up with good domestic habits, they should have, as one means of securing the result, a neat and cheerful kitchen. A kitchen should always, if possible, be entirely above-ground, and well lighted . . . if flowers and shrubs be cultivated around the doors and windows . . . it will add very much to their agreeable appearance."

The authors advocated a small, efficient kitchen, such as a cook's galley found on steamships and pointed out that "in most large houses, the table furniture, the cooking material and utensils, the sink, and the eating-room, are at such distances apart, that half the time and strength is employed in walking back and forth to collect and return the articles used."

Catherine Beecher and Harriet Beecher Stowe suggested the well-equipped kitchen should contain numerous items, including redware and stoneware for storing staples; ironware pots, pans, waffle iron, and kettle; tinware pans for baking; and utensils such as an apple corer, egg boiler, sugar scoops, a set of mugs, scales and weights, colander, large and small grater, and so on. They also recommended the kitchen contain woodenware tubs, pails, beetle for mashing potatoes, breadboard, egg beater, saltbox, and spice boxes. Baskets also should be available for collecting eggs and fruit and for shopping.

During the late 1800s the Industrial Revolution continued to influence home life. By the 1870s indoor plumbing made it possible and more appealing to build kitchens and adjoining workrooms on the first floors of homes and townhouses. These kitchens of the late 1800s had a crisp, sanitary appearance, featuring a white porcelain sink, white tile wainscoting on the walls, white cupboards with glass doors, and cool quarry tile or wood flooring. The large coal/woodburning cast-iron stove and wooden icebox were the modern appliances of the day.

As the nineteenth century drew to a close, the majority of middle-class women found themselves spending long hours in the kitchen. Young immigrant girls were leaving their positions as hired help to seek employment in the new factories and service-oriented businesses. As a result the mistress of the house was left to run the kitchen alone. Women voiced their objection to devoting their entire day to kitchen chores, and industry responded

A 1924 advertisement by the Hoosier Mfg. Co., Newcastle, Ind., depicting the completely and tastefully furnished kitchen.

A 1926 advertisement for Armstrong linoleum features a colorful kitchen with color in the flooring, furniture, curtains, walls, and accessories.

by flooding the market with more packaged foods and numerous patented gadgets and utensils designed to make life easier. Necessity was no longer the only catalyst behind innovation. *Convenience* became a key word for the new century.

After 1900 efforts to modernize the kitchen gave women many small appliances and step-saving, multipurpose concentrated work centers. The new century brought with it a preference for an all-inclusive, downsized kitchen where everything would be at hand. The popular Hoosier-style kitchen cabinet served as a minipantry and worktable all in one and was the forerunner of continuous built-in kitchen counters and cabinets.

While an all-electric kitchen was featured at the 1893 Chicago World's Fair, it wasn't until the early 1900s that electric appliances were being used in a small number of homes. Once power plants and distribution systems were available to

standardize electric currents, every type of electric appliance or gadget imaginable was being patented and sold.

The kitchen of the 1920s and 1930s no longer resembled the sanitary white kitchen popular at the turn of the century. The introduction of color into both the room itself and all types of kitchenware, along with *streamlined* designs and continued advances in electrical appliances, combined to give new meaning to the word *modernization*.

The November 1934 issue of *Needlecraft—The Home Arts Magazine* featured an article entitled "Kitchens of Today," by Agnes Heisler Barton. She wrote, "Color and line have become a part of this once humble room and now it is the most modern room of the house."

As the "most modern room of the house," the kitchen of 1934 was the focus of widespread attention. Exhibits displaying kitchens were quite popular at that time, and the article went on to tell readers about an exhibit of six kitchens,

154-806

The kitchen of 1934 with GE Monitor Top refrigerator, electric stove, and Hoosier kitchen cabinet. Courtesy of GE Appliance Historical Archives.

made in miniature, that illustrated the changes in the kitchen over the past century.

The first miniature, Agnes Barton wrote, "showed a kitchen of the year 1833 when cooking was done in an iron kettle over the fireplace . . . earthenware dishes were in an open cupboard . . . candles were used for illumination."

The second kitchen was the "kitchen of 1860 when stoves were built into the fireplace and the first crude zinc sink appeared . . . kitchen floors of white pine had to be scrubbed daily."

In the kitchen of 1888, "a new gas stove is the significant development of that day in kitchen equipment . . . progress is also shown in the iron sink."

The fourth kitchen displayed "an amusing suburban kitchen of the year 1900. Improvements that came in with the new century were a work table equipped with flour bins, a kitchen cabinet, an improved gas stove, white enameled sink with drainboards and white tile used as wainscoting . . . wood trim and furniture in this kitchen were of golden oak."

"In the fifth kitchen, dated 1920, the white marquisette curtains, blue and white tile floor, dining alcove and French Provincial furniture reflected the awakening interest in interior decoration."

The last miniature Agnes Heisler Barton wrote about was a model of the modern 1934 kitchen. "It was fitted up with the last word in labor-saving devices, automatic refrigerator, stove with

The modern 1950 kitchen with state-of-the-art electric stove, refrigerator, dishwasher and streamlined cupboards and countertops. Courtesy of GE Appliance Historical Archives.

thermostatic control...rubber-tile flooring—all arranged so as to avoid wasted energy and unnecessary work."

Since 1934, kitchens have continued to become more modern, with the introduction of chrome and plastics in the 1940s and 1950s, and further improvements in design and technology that ultimately have led to the sleek, state-of-the-art kitchen of the 1990s.

The vast array of collectible kitchenware from the 1800s through the 1940s (with interest growing in kitchenware items from the 1950s and 1960s) substantiates the fact that collectors appreciate the importance of preserving these tools of domestic, social, and historical significance.

CHAPTER 1 Advertising Memorabilia

Old advertising memorabilia is recognized as a colorful and highly collectible art form. The concept of advertising emerged during the eighteenth century, when miracle cures and assorted home remedies were being promoted in town and village newspapers. The early 1800s saw these remedies being sold in embossed bottles bearing the manufacturer's name.

Throughout the nineteenth century commercial goods expanded to include various products that could be purchased for home use. At the same time there were advances in advertising and printing techniques and the use of more modern machinery to produce the tins and boxes for commercial goods. These containers pioneered further advertisements featuring giveaways, promotional items, and product premiums.

In the area of kitchen-related advertising memorabilia, today's collector looks for advertising giveaways, product tins and boxes, advertising cookbooks and household almanacs, souvenir spoons, and bottles.

Some advertising campaigns, such as those by Coca-Cola, were so massive and popular that today collectors specialize in one product memorabilia. Other noted advertisements included Dr Pepper, Hires, Log Cabin syrup, Moxie, and Pepsi-Cola.

Advertising Tins and Boxes

Product packaging from the late 1800s through the 1940s is a highly sought-after kitchen collectible. These old containers were used for the commercial sale of food, beverages, spices, and other commodities.

Metal containers first were used to package goods in England in the 1700s. During the early 1800s this practice made its way to the United States, and by the

Late 1800s japanned tea tin, orange and black with floral decoration, 9″ high by 7½″ wide, $75.00.

Coffee tin with white, green, and red paper label, "Perfection Coffee D.C. Heuer, Roasted & Packed for D.C. Heuer, Dealer in Fancy Groceries, Choice Meats & Dry Goods, Bergholz, N.Y.," 6″ tall, $30.00.

1830s certain fruits and vegetables were commercially packaged in these handmade containers.

The canning industry rapidly expanded as a result of the Civil War. Both Van Camp and Libby, familiar names to-

Attractive and rare 1-pound coffee tin, yellow decoration, 7″ tall by 3½″ wide, $125.00.

Rectangular ½-pound tea tin, red with gold and black lettering, 6″ wide by 2¼″ high, $10.00.

KYBO ½-pound coffee tin, white and red, 6″ tall by 3″ wide, $29.00.

day, began canning by mechanized means in the 1860s and 1870s. These canned goods were a time-saving modern convenience.

American manufacturers of tin containers included the American Stopper Company, Brooklyn, New York; Ginna and Company, New York City; and Somers Brothers, Brooklyn, New York. The American Can Company, Maywood, Illinois, founded in 1901, bought out these other companies by 1905.

In the second half of the 1800s, the advent of the printing process called lithography meant pictures no longer had to be black-and-white line drawings, as they had been since colonial times. Now containers could be decorated with lifelike color images on paper labels.

The 1880s saw further advancements in printing. Chromolithography, a process by which color pictures could be printed directly on a tin plate, allowed artists and designers (employed by many companies) to create attractive packaging.

On much of the advertising memor-abilia available today, the style and design can be an accurate indication of age and a reflection of marketing techniques. For example, Victorian and art nouveau art work and art deco "cubist" designs were used on containers, and each has its own characteristics.

Of the various tins used for packaging kitchen-related goods, collectors often search for tea, coffee, baking powder, and spice containers.

COFFEE, TEA, AND SPICE TINS

Prior to the 1920s coffee and tea were sold in tin containers of all shapes and sizes. The 1910 Montgomery Ward *Groceries Price List* catalog offered coffee in a decorative 3-pound cylinder-shaped tin

French tea tin (THÉ), 6½″ tall, $18.00.

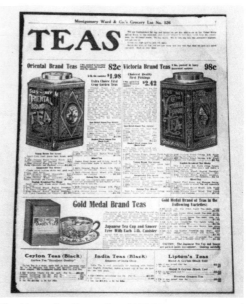

The November/December 1910 Montgomery Ward and Company's Grocery List No. 526 catalog offered Oriental Brand Teas in very decorative 5-pound tins.

Tea tin, "Chase & Sanborn Teas are also Delicious," 5″ tall by 4½″ wide, $5.00.

Tea tin, red, green, and yellow, 7″ tall by 4″ wide, $30.00.

and 5-pound rectangular tin. They also offered their customers a free fancy cake tin box with the $3.53 purchase of 15 pounds of roasted coffee.

Montgomery Ward and Company advertised "not only do we lead the world in the high quality and fair prices of our coffees, but we also lead in the valuable receptacles that we give you with your coffee purchases." The 15 pounds of coffee were shipped inside the large cake tin, which was finished in green with decorative gold bronze stenciling.

The same 1910 Montgomery Ward catalog also sold Oriental Brand Teas in "two pound and five pound handsomely

11

Watkins allspice tin, 3¼ ounces, 3½" tall, $22.50.

One-pound Manru coffee can, yellow with red and black print, 6½" tall by 4" wide, $32.00.

Three Crow mustard tin, 3 ounces, yellow with red lettering, 4" tall by 2¼" wide, $36.00.

decorated tin canisters that will last a lifetime for pantry uses."

Victoria Brand Teas were sold in "two pound and five pound decorated, Old English style tea canisters. Every housewife will be delighted with the canister," proclaimed the catalog. Victoria Brand Tea tins were very ornate and featured lithographed designs.

By the late 1920s coffee and tea were available in standard 1-, 2-, and 3-pound cans. They often were decorated with colorful lithographed designs, and many were marketed by popular grocery companies.

Assorted spices, baking powder, mustard, and extracts were made by many companies from the mid-1800s on, and these tins also are highly collectible.

Philadelphia's Colburn's Spices was established in 1857 and sold mustard, spices, cooking herbs, and pickling spices in tins.

The J.R. Watkins Company of Winona, Minnesota, founded in 1868, sold a full line of spices packaged in tins with lift-top lids. They marketed and sold their products through a direct-sell method, employing hundreds of traveling salesmen.

Other nineteenth-century companies

Lipton's coffee, 1-pound can, yellow with red and white lettering, "1920 by Thomas Lipton Inc., in the U.S. of America," rare and unusual, $60.00.

Stickney and Poor's mustard tin, green and black paper label with white lettering and red horseshoe, 5″ tall by 3″ wide, $48.00.

Staley's baking powder tin, "¼ pound" contents, 3¼″ tall, $22.50.

Durkee's cream tartar, circa 1893, light green paper label with green and red lettering, 4½″ tall by 3″ wide, $12.50.

A&P spice tin, red with gold lettering, 1½ ounce, 3″ tall, $35.00.

marketing spices in decorative tins included McCormick and Company, which was established in 1889; Stickney and Poor's, established in 1815; and Durkee, which began operation in 1857.

By the 1930s the spoon lift-top lid was being used on spice tins and continues to be used today.

Baking powder also has been packaged and sold since the mid-nineteenth century, but this often was sold in a glass container until the 1880s. Royal Baking Powder always was packaged in tin, but others, such as Arm and Hammer and Calumet, first used glass.

Along with collecting tins by product, some collectors look for containers produced by specific manufacturers. For example, Somers Brothers of Brooklyn, New York, were first in producing chromolithographed containers. Their decorative tins are highly collectible.

Tins remain available for collecting today because our thrifty and practical

Celluloid starch box (never opened), 5″ tall by 3½″ wide, $8.00.

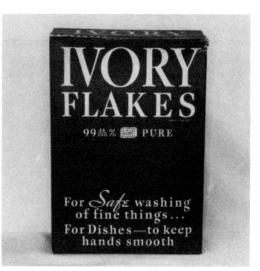

Ivory Flakes soapbox (never opened), blue with white lettering, 8½″ tall by 6″ wide, $5.00.

Back of Ivory Flakes soapbox with instructions for washing everything from dishes to woolens.

Egg box, ½ dozen, 6″ wide by 2¼″ high by 4″ deep, $8.00.

ancestors put these containers to some other use once they were emptied of their original contents. Watch for tins to turn up at house sales, flea markets, auctions, antiques shops, and especially at those antiques shows that specialize in advertising memorabilia.

BOXES

Box manufacturing originated in London, England, in the early 1800s. These boxes were oval or round and most often were used to store hats or package chocolates and assorted pills. Boxes for commercial packaging of goods were being used in the United States by the late 1800s.

Lithography provided for colorful advertising designs on boxes, just as with tin containers. Commercial products such as Quaker oats and Morton salt were packaged in these cardboard boxes and still are today.

Other notable products packaged in appealing boxes include Cracker Jack, which was being sold in boxes by 1896. In 1912 prizes were put into Cracker Jack boxes, and the familiar Cracker Jack boy became the advertising symbol for this product in 1925.

Another popular package is the round blue box that contains Morton salt. This packaging has been used since 1911, and women all across the country became familiar with the slogan "When It Rains It Pours" and the little girl with the umbrella.

In a full-page advertisement in the March 14, 1925, *Saturday Evening Post*, the Package Machinery Company of Springfield, Massachusetts, stated "that all successful packages are wrapped in printed or transparent wrappers is no mere coincidence—for that is the way to protect the product and give it that increased sales value which comes from making the package attractive."

Among their list of customers, Package Machinery Company included Walter Baker and Company Ltd., Beech-Nut Packing Company, Borden's Condensed Milk Company, National Biscuit Company, Postum Cereal Company, and Shredded Wheat Company.

Early boxes are quite rare and often command a higher price than tin containers. Unfortunately, they have not survived the years as well as tin packaging has because they most often were discarded or have decayed. Common examples available today date from the 1930s and 1940s and include soapboxes, cereal boxes, and oatmeal packaging. Look for these boxes at antiques shops and shows, especially from those dealers who specialize in kitchenware or advertising memorabilia.

Advertising Gadgets and Giveaways

When the Industrial Revolution ushered in numerous new products, businesses, and services, growing companies across the country were competing for the patronage of new consumers.

Early black-and-white trade card, a forerunner of the advertising giveaway, $1.00.

Advertising giveaway marked "Niagara County National Bank, Lockport, NY," 12" long, $7.00.

The history of advertising chronicles the introduction of several ideas aimed at capturing the public's attention, including the giveaway.

What began in the second half of the nineteenth century with the distribution of colorful advertising trade cards quickly progressed to the free distribution of assorted kitchen- and household-related items bearing the company's name or slogan.

One late nineteenth-century company who used giveaways prolifically was the C.D. Kenny Company. This retail and wholesale grocery chain gave away many advertising items during the 1890s to 1930s, including kitchenware items such as tea strainers, extension sifters, assorted spoons, and decorative spice tins.

In 1934 C.D. Kenny's retail grocery stores closed, ending the era of the Kenny giveaways.

Perhaps no other company has given away as many advertising items as the Coca-Cola Company. Developed in 1886 by a Georgia pharmacist, Coca-Cola immediately began a full-scale advertising campaign. Over the years their bottle openers and ice picks have become popular kitchen (and Coca-Cola) collectibles.

Thousands of companies have offered customers numerous kitchen-related giveaways from 1890 to the 1940s. Some of the more popular collectibles include tea strainers, funnels, tins, glasses, mugs, teapots, dishes, match safes, cookie cutters, pot scrapers, and an assortment of gadgets and utensils.

Matchbox holders were another popular advertising giveaway. Made of tin or cast iron and bearing an advertisement, this necessary kitchenware item usually was hung next to the stove and the matches were used for lighting fires. Although book matches were developed in the 1930s, match safes still were being used well into the 1940s in rural areas.

With the invention of William Painter's metal crown bottle seal in 1892 came a need for another kitchen gadget: the bottle opener. Businesses wasted no time in pressing bottle openers into service as giveaways. While one end of the opener served to remove the crown seal bottle cap, the other end was given an assortment of uses, such as ice pick or spoon.

Another kitchenware item distributed as a giveaway was the egg separator. Designed to separate the yolk and egg white, these factory-produced gadgets were made of tin or aluminum and bore an embossed advertisement or slogan for stove companies, baking powder and spice manufacturers, and others.

Ice picks usually were distributed by refrigerator manufacturers, ironworks plants, and ice companies. Ice picks were made of steel with cast-iron or hardwood handles. Picks with a hardwood handle

Advertising measuring spoon, "Schrack Coal, level full, quarter cup," $4.00.

Enameled advertising cup, white with blue lettering, "Dickinson's 'Ace' Clover Seed Co," 3″ tall, $35.00.

Advertising pinchers, "D&H Coal, Donaldson Co., Inc.," $2.00.

Advertising matchbox safe, 6½" tall, $25.00.

Advertising bottle opener with cottage cheese spoon, "Onondaga Milk Products—Cottage Cheese—Syracuse, NY," 11" long, $12.00.

Tin egg separator, "Howard E. Lane Pharmacist, Walton, NY," $14.00.

often had a tinned cap on the end. These kitchen tools were used until electric refrigeration became commonplace in the 1940s.

Another common giveaway was the measuring cup. A necessary kitchenware item, crystal (clear glass) measuring cups most often were given by coffee and tea companies, flour and spice companies, and furniture manufacturers.

Pottery dishes, children's plates, mugs, cups and saucers, bowls, creamers and sugars, and servers were distributed as advertising giveaways through the 1940s. They were given away by furniture companies, insurance companies, grocery stores, appliance dealers, dry cleaners, banks, gas stations, and bakeries and were produced by well-noted potteries such as Hall China Company, Harker Pottery Company, Homer Laughlin China Company, and others.

Collectors will find that advertising giveaways can turn up almost anywhere, but the hard-to-come-by items usually are found at antiques shows specializing in advertising memorabilia. The condition of the item, the product it represents, and rarity will all have an impact on pricing in this area of collecting.

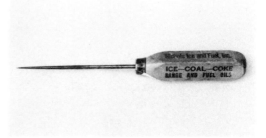

Ice pick, "Nichols Ice and Fuel, Inc., Ice—Coal—Coke, Range and Fuel Oils," 8½" long, $5.00.

Advertising fly swatter, "F.L. Grants Complete Furnishing House," Salamanca, N.Y., 14" long, $12.00.

Advertising measuring glass, "PHOSPHO-SODA Fleet Buffered Laxative—Acts Within One Hour or Overnight," 3½″ tall, $10.00.

Early 1900s advertising cookbook, *The Enterprising Housekeeper*, by the Enterprise Manufacturing Company, $2.00.

Advertising coffee mug, "This is a World Famous Horn & Hardart Automat," 3¾″ tall, $10.00.

COOKBOOKS AND HOUSEHOLD ALMANACS

Advertising cookbooks were printed and distributed as one of the numerous advertising giveaways from the 1890s through the 1940s. They usually were distributed by companies involved in food production, kitchen appliances, or cooking.

These advertising cookbooks offer a glimpse at the domestic concerns of the day and views on health and nutrition. Others noted the popular response to these giveaways or premiums, and by the turn of the century many different companies were offering cookbooks to their customers. For example, the Metropolitan Life Insurance Company issued several advertising cookbooks during the early 1900s.

Advertising cookbooks increasingly are being recognized as a significant advertising collectible/kitchen collectible. Millions were distributed, and they often were saved and used for favorite recipes; they are easy for collectors to find and

Advertising lunch box, circa 1910, red and black with handles on either side, "Tiger Tobacco," 8″ wide by 6″ tall, $50.00.

The back of *The Enterprising Housekeeper* depicts four of the Enterprise Manufacturing Company's early kitchenwares.

Advertising cookbook published by the Metropolitan Life Insurance Company, "This book has been prepared to help the housewife in her everlasting question, What shall I have for dinner tonite?" $2.00.

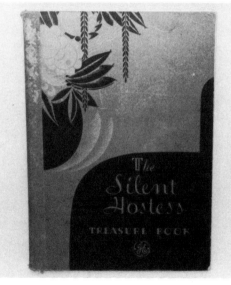

The 1932 General Electric *The Silent Hostess Treasure Book*, $1.00.

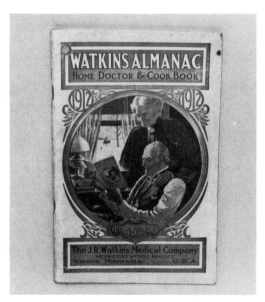

The 1912 *Watkins Almanac Home Doctor & Cook Book*, by the J.R. Watkins Medical Company, Winona, Minn., $8.00.

remain inexpensive. Expect pre-1900 cookbooks and cookbooks shaped like the product they advertise to cost more.

Household almanacs also were distributed by many companies and enjoyed widespread popularity between the late 1800s and the 1940s. Most household al-

manacs contained monthly calendars, astrological information, and home remedies. Others, such as *J.R. Watkins Almanac*, made by the Watkins Company of Winona, Minnesota, also included a variety of recipes that called for Watkins spices and flavorings.

This almanac also served as a catalog, because J.R. Watkins was a direct-sales company that employed door-to-door salesmen. Although the company is still in business today, the almanac was discontinued around 1940.

SOUVENIR SPOONS

Souvenir spoons can be considered a form of early advertising. Popular from the 1890s through the 1920s, these attractive collectibles initially were created by silversmiths and jewelers as souvenirs of historical sites, resorts, large cities, and even buildings.

Souvenir spoons had their beginning in Washington, D.C., in 1889. M. W. Galt designed the first souvenir spoon based on a ladle used by George Washington. Galt's spoon bore a medallion of George Washington and was issued in May 1889 by the Galt firm. More than 10,000 spoons were sold in its first year.

Although Galt actually designed one of the first American-made souvenir spoons, it was a New England silversmith that successfully launched their popularity. In 1890, Daniel Low created a spoon featuring Salem, Massachusetts. It actually was Low's son, Seth, who designed this spoon, which recalled Salem's history of witchcraft trials. The spoon bore the design of a witch clutching her broomstick and the word *Salem*.

Low advertised his souvenir spoon in the *Saturday Evening Post*, and this first spoon became so popular that the father-and-son team created and marketed a second design.

Other silversmiths and jewelers noted the popularity of these souvenir spoons and began creating their own. Although these early spoons were made of sterling silver, later manufacturers made silver-plated souvenir spoons, some featuring colored enamel decorations.

While most souvenir spoons were teaspoon-size, they also were sold and offered as premiums in the form of coffee

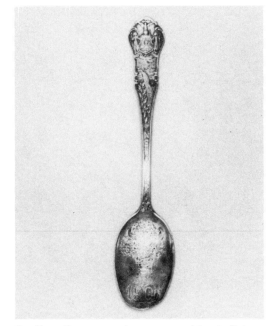

Sterling silver souvenir teaspoon with a buffalo head on the spoon, "New York 1901," $18.00.

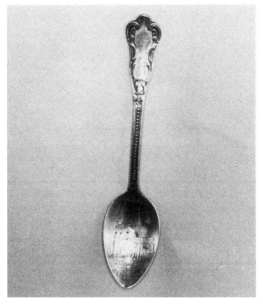

Sterling silver child's souvenir spoon, "Catholic Church, Wellsville, N.Y.," $12.00.

spoons, soup spoons, demitasse spoons, and children's spoons.

So many different themes exist today that collectors usually seek spoons in one area. Souvenir spoons also are collected by manufacturer (the Gorham Corpora-

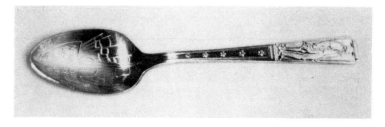

Souvenir teaspoon by National Silver Company, "New York World's Fair 1939," $20.00.

tion was the largest producer of souvenir spoons in the United States) and by size.

Many older souvenir spoons remain available for collecting today, and new ones still are being issued. They require little space, are reasonably priced, and are as popular today as they were with the Victorians. Souvenir spoons are one of the first true collectibles.

BOTTLES

Identified as one of the first forms of product advertisement, old bottles make an interesting and colorful collection.

Early glassworks companies were established in the 1700s, and by the mid-nineteenth century, many were operating throughout New England and Ohio. The South Lyndeboro Glass Company of New Hampshire was established in 1866. They produced many of the bottles that collectors seek today, such as Mason canning jars. (For more information on canning jars, see Chapter 8.) Lyndeboro glass most often was produced in robin's-egg blue, which was a shade unique to this company. Many of their bottles also were made in aqua blue and dark amber.

There are many types of old bottles available for collecting, and age can be important in determining value. Both pontil marks and mold seams on bottles can accurately indicate age. The pontil mark is a circular depressed area with sharp edges that results from the glassblower removing the tool, or pontil, that holds the glass during the finishing stages of manufacturing. Such a mark indicates that a bottle was made before 1860. During the 1860s the widespread use of molds

Mineral Springs water bottle, 14″ tall, $15.00.

Glass creamer with original tin cap, 1-pint size, 7″ tall, $15.00.

21

Two quart bottles, embossed "Heuer's Model Dairy, Good Morning & Good Health," 8″ tall, each $5.00.

French Lipton milk bottle, red and yellow painted slogan, 10″ tall, $48.00.

to make bottles left a seam on the finished product. By 1904 the Libbey Glass Company of Toledo, Ohio, had so perfected their bottle-making machine that the seam then ran to the very top of the bottle.

Bottles were made throughout the years to package kitchen products such as soda, mineral water, vinegar, milk, nursing milk, extracts, and flavorings.

Milk bottles are popular collectibles that were used widely from 1900 to 1950. They often are considered a regional item and were made in assorted sizes with either an embossed or painted dairy name and/or slogan. With rare exceptions, most milk bottles can be had for a very small investment.

Collectors also look for embossed bottles of other products and figurals and bottles with paper labels intact. Antiques shows that specialize in advertising memorabilia are an especially good market for bottle collectors, and auctions, flea markets, and house sales also can provide excellent finds.

CHAPTER 2 Appliances Large and Small

When we think of large kitchen appliances today, we include the stove, refrigerator, microwave, and dishwasher. Smaller everyday appliances we depend on include food processors, blenders, coffee makers, toasters, and other state-of-the-art electrical necessities.

The nineteenth-century housewife achieved limited freedom from kitchen chores with the advent of her own modern appliances.

In 1869, F.A. Walker and Company of Boston, Massachusetts, advertised their Kitchen Furnishing Emporium in the *Boston Directory*. The emporium sold imported European goods, refrigerators, water coolers, ice cream freezers, and other assorted merchandise.

Other emporiums, wholesale dealers, tinsmiths, ironworkers, and mail-order catalogs offered customers cooking stoves, iron sets, and primitive toasters.

After the turn of the century, the kitchen was the focus of technological and industrial advances that altered domestic engineering.

The early 1900s saw the introduction of numerous electric household appliances and gadgets, and by the 1930s electric utilities had expanded and standardized to such an extent that electricity was available in most homes.

A 1918 Landers, Frary and Clark advertisement for their Universal line of electrical appliances included a chafing dish, toaster, coffeepot, waffle iron, and clothing iron. By the late 1920s improvements such as timers and heat regulators were being added to these and other appliances.

The 1920s and 1930s also saw the introduction of small appliances such as electric roasters, corn poppers, egg cookers, and electric mixers that also could serve as juice squeezers, mincers, flour sifters, graters, and knife sharpeners.

Iceboxes and Refrigerators

Thanks to the advent of industrialization, the late nineteenth-century homemaker had the advantage of indoor refrigeration. Although a box on the back porch or the window ledge would suffice in keeping perishables cold during the win-

Wooden-handled sadiron,
6″ long, $25.00.

Oak icebox, the Baldwin Refrigerator Co., Burlington, Vt., 38″ tall by 27″ wide, $595.00

A 1919 advertisement for Leonard's Refrigerator by the Grand Rapids Refrigerator Co. of Grand Rapids, Mich. This model was lined with porcelain for easy cleaning.

ter, the heat of the summer months created problems in trying to keep food from spoiling.

The ice industry, in full swing by the mid-1800s, led to the development of the icebox by the 1860s. From the 1860s through the early 1900s, different styles and sizes of wooden iceboxes were available for use in the kitchen or pantry.

"The iceman may need the money and the plumber may need the work— but neither is reason for using an ice-eater of a refrigerator.... You want a refrigerator that is sanitary, safe, and saving," proclaimed a 1910 advertisement for Belding-Hall Company refrigerators.

Belding-Hall, of Belding, Michigan, was one of many companies that combined a means of insulation with the theory of circulation (warm air rises to the top, sending the cold air down into the food compartment) to produce iceboxes.

Other manufacturers included Baldwin Refrigerator Company, Burlington, Vermont; Eureka Refrigerator Company, Indianapolis, Indiana; John C. Jewett

Manufacturing Company, Buffalo, New York; Monroe Refrigerator Company, Lockland, Ohio; Northern Refrigerator Company, Grand Rapids, Michigan; and White Enamel Refrigerator Company, St. Paul, Minnesota.

These iceboxes were made of oak, elm, ash, or pine and typically had a golden oak finish. They were available in different sizes and styles, from plain to very ornate. They were accessorized with brass hinges and locks.

The interior of the icebox was lined with metal, zinc, or porcelain to insulate the appliance and help maintain sanitary conditions. The icebox had a drainage pipe to carry water from the melting ice block either outdoors or into a pan that the everwatchful housewife or cook would empty before it overflowed.

In the early 1900s an icebox could be purchased for a few dollars for a small model, upward to $25.00 for a large, decorative one. The 1908 Sears Roebuck catalog advertised their "Economy Refrigerators" for $4.45 to $17.95. These refrigerators were promoted as "an excellent preserver of food with an economical consumption of ice."

The wooden icebox quickly evolved into the electric refrigerator. Industrialization and modernization resulted in many changes during the early 1900s. By the late 1920s the wooden icebox was becoming obsolete.

ELECTRIC REFRIGERATORS

General Electric introduced their Monitor Top refrigerator in 1927. One of their advertisements stated "Now Comes—Simplified Electric Refrigeration." This porcelain-over-steel unit had a motor "housed in a hermetically sealed casing mounted on top of the cabinet. . . . You never need oil it . . . it uses very little current and no special wiring is needed to hook it up—the regular house current is adequate."

General Electric offered a five-year warranty on the Monitor Top and first-year sales figures were very impressive.

Further improvements from General Electric included a refrigerator designed with a separate freezer compartment in 1929, the invention of an insulation called Thermocraft in 1931, and the use of adjustable shelves in refrigerators in 1933.

In a 1936 full-page advertisement in *Good Housekeeping* magazine, General Electric reported "The new General Electric models offer all the latest convenience features: handy temperature control and defrosting switch, sliding shelves, automatic interior lighting, foot-pedal door opener, quick releasing ice trays, stainless-steel super-freezer, vegetable compartment, and stainless porcelain interiors with rounded corners."

Although General Electric was the leading manufacturer of electric refrigerators, other companies were producing these appliances too, including familiar

A 1927 advertisement for the GE Monitor Top electric refrigerator. Courtesy of GE Appliance Historical Archives.

This 1936 Westinghouse refrigerator was advertised in the May 1936 *Good Housekeeping* magazine. Although the design is still boxlike, the corners are rounded.

names like Kelvinator, Frigidaire, White House, Philco, Westinghouse, and Admiral.

Styles slowly began to change during the 1930s and 1940s. The boxlike refrigerators of the previous decade began to appear with rounded corners. The appli-

A 1939 GE refrigerator with a more modern look and rounded corners. Courtesy of GE Appliance Historical Archives.

ance was made larger and the high legs popular on some models disappeared. The refrigerators of the 1940s had a modernistic design and boasted numerous convenience features.

Although the old wooden icebox is eagerly sought after by antiques and collectibles enthusiasts, there has been little demand for examples of early electric refrigeration. This will no doubt change as the interest in early electric appliances and gadgets continues to grow.

Look for wooden iceboxes at auctions, antiques shops and shows, and estate sales. The price will be determined by the condition, size, style, demand, and sometimes the manufacturer. Early electric refrigerators were extremely heavy and, therefore, are not very portable. Collectors should check with antiques dealers who have an interest in early electric appliances and antiques or appliance columns of newspapers and "items-for-sale" publications.

Irons

Cast-iron sadirons at one time served to perform the most tedious of household tasks. Made of heavy cast iron, the sadirons we find today were factory made in large quantities in the 1800s. They came in several different weights, with handles attached in two spots on a triangular base.

These irons were heated on the stove or by the open fire, and posed the threat of serious burns until a practical woman named Mrs. Potts designed square-backed and double-pointed irons with removeable wooden handles.

Mrs. Potts's irons were available in sets that included three or more irons, a detachable handle, and a trivet. These sets, manufactured by the Enterprise Manufacturing Company, were packaged in attractive wooden boxes and sold for $1.12 on up. They were sold at hardware and home-furnishing stores and were advertised as "a convenient article for the tidy housekeeper and a tasty, suitable present always appreciable."

By the year 1900, hollow irons were being manufactured; a heated slug would be inserted in the hollow to warm the iron. Just three years later a man named Earl Richardson invented an electric iron with a "hot point," which launched the Hotpoint trade name in appliances.

In 1904, General Electric manufactured an electric iron, but the use of electricity was limited to so few areas that it would be another thirty years before the electric iron gained in popularity. In the meantime, gasoline and kerosene irons with fuel tanks were marketed and sold, but were quite unsafe because of the risk of fire and explosion.

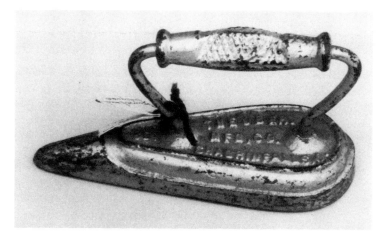

Sadiron, "The Ober. Mfg. Co. Chagrin Falls, Ohio," 6½" long, $49.00.

Mrs. Potts double-pointed iron with removable wooden handle, 6½" long, $18.00.

Sadiron, 6" long, $10.00.

Hotpoint Calrod electric iron by GE, circa 1920s, "Volts 115, Watts 660, Cat. #149F86," 8" long, $6.50.

Coleman gas iron, baby blue enamelware finish with wooden handle, 9″ long, $40.00.

Steam-O-Matic Iron by the Steam-O-Matic Corp. of Milwaukee, Wis., circa 1930s, aluminum, "115 Volts A.C. or D.C., Pat. Pending., Model No. D-550," 10″ long, $18.50.

The 1924 Montgomery Ward catalog offered a set of Mrs. Potts's sadirons for $1.39, a set of three cast-iron flat irons (6, 7, and 8 pounds) for $1.79, a charcoal iron for $2.10, a Superior Safe gasoline iron for $5.19, and the Hotpoint electric iron with 6-foot cord and plug for $5.25.

In 1931 an advertisement for the Coleman Lamp and Stove Company gasoline iron told readers, "On ironing day just scratch a match, light your iron and in a few minutes you are ready to start ironing! No tramping from stove to ironing board, no hot stove to keep going.

Two models, both handsomely finished in colors, with nickel trimmings."

By the 1930s several electric irons were being manufactured, including the 1930 Mysto model, which featured the first temperature control.

In 1933, Proctor electrical appliances included the Automatic Heat-Adjusting Speed Iron with a temperature-control dial that included settings for different fabrics. An off switch was an added feature on this same iron. The 6-pound, 1,000-watt model sold for $8.50 and the 4½-pound, 1,000-watt model cost $8.00.

The following year Proctor and Schwartz Electric Company of Philadelphia, Pennsylvania, introduced the Magic Stand Iron. A 1934 company catalog stated "the novel stand swings under the iron at the touch of a button, and springs out of the way again the instant ironing is resumed. . . . The MAGIC STAND gives magical relief from the arm fatigue of lifting an iron the length of the board to a separate stand."

Other companies that manufactured early electric irons include Westinghouse; Waring Products; The Knapp-Monarch Company; Landers, Frary and Clark; and Manning-Bowman Appliances.

The electric iron of the 1940s was sleek, streamlined, and had the added feature of providing steam. For example, the Proctor Electric Deluxe Never Lift was a modernistic early 1940s iron that not only had the Proctor automatic stand, but also boasted a headlight, fabric dial, speed selector, and built-in cord. An additional "steamer" (steam attachment) also was available; this was plugged into an electrical outlet, then held in place on the side of the ironing board while a fabric-covered tube was attached to the iron. An on/off switch on the iron controlled the steam.

By the end of the decade steam came from a water reservoir attached directly to the iron and new, sleeker models continued to be designed.

The 1948 Sunbeam Ironmaster was a state-of-the-art model advertised as being "hot in 30 seconds." Their advertisement stated, "until you've used Sunbeam Ironmaster, you've no idea how much faster and easier ironing can be. . . . You finish quicker, feeling fresher with a Sunbeam."

By 1950, with a uniform distribution of electric power available to even the most rural households, the electric iron had replaced the earlier sadirons and coal and gasoline irons.

Westinghouse electric iron, late 1940s, "Adjust-O-Matic Steam Iron, Mansfield, Ohio," 9" long, $6.50.

Old irons turn up almost anywhere, from yard sales to antiques shows, and there is an increasing interest in early electric models.

Stoves

Large cast-iron ranges maintained their popularity throughout the late 1800s. Although small, freestanding Franklin stoves continued to be used for cooking and heat, the larger high-back ranges offered cooks more convenience in preparing their meals.

The large cast-iron stove of the late 1800s could burn wood, coal, corncobs, or any combination of these for fuel. These stoves were capable of roasting meat, warming bread, and keeping water warm in a reservoir. Many of these vintage cookstoves were decorated with ornate nickel trim.

In 1920 the Weir Stove Company of Taunton, Massachusetts, advertised their Gold Medal Glenwood, which could do every kind of cooking and was fueled by gas or coal/wood. This particular stove had separate sections for either type of fuel and, all told, had three ovens and nine burners.

Many different companies manufactured the popular cast-iron stove, includ-

31

A 1920 advertisement for the Sanico coal-/wood-/gas-burning porcelain range.

A 1920 advertisement for Hughes Electric stove by Edison Electric Appliance Co., Chicago, Ill.

ing the United States Stove Company, South Pittsburg, Tennessee; Eclipse Stove Company, Mansfield, Ohio; Weir Stove Company, Taunton, Massachusetts; Cleveland Metal Products Company, Cleveland, Ohio; Central Oil and Gas Stove Company, Gardner, Massachusetts; American Range and Foundry Company, Chicago, Illinois; and Phillips and Clark Stoves Company, Geneva, New York.

In the early 1920s, Hotpoint developed a white porcelain finish for their stoves, which was quite a change from the black cast iron used until then. By the end of the decade porcelain-finished stoves were available in a variety of colors or with a pastel trim. Not only were they easy to clean, but they also often introduced the first bit of color into an otherwise drab kitchen. For example, the United States Stove Company offered their Avalon Delux Balanced Range coal- or oil-burning stoves in an all-white porcelain enamel finish, ivory with green panels, and ivory with tan panels.

The 1920s also saw serious development of the electric range, but because so many households were without electricity or had only limited electric power, these stoves didn't gain in popularity until the 1930s.

An early advertisement for the Hughes Electric Range (with four burners, oven, and warming oven) by Edison Electric Appliance Company, Inc., advised readers "when you build your house be sure enough convenience outlets are provided so you can freely use electrical household appliances."

The 1930s ushered in the streamlined stove. No longer did the stove sit on high legs—the new tabletop ranges fit flush with counters and sinks. The cooking now was done on top of the stove with a single oven below, available in gas or electric. For example, Hotpoint intro-

This 1930 advertisement depicts the Patrician Magic Chef gas range with "Italian Grand Antique Marble Finish," ivory trim, and an oven heat regulator. This top-of-the-line model sold for $195.00 new.

A 1931 GE/Hotpoint electric stove with an automatic timer, light, and "range set" with salt and pepper and clock. Courtesy of GE Appliance Historical Archives.

The 1934 cabinet-style stove with drawers for storing pots and pans. Courtesy of GE Appliance Historical Archives.

duced their cabinet model stove in 1934. Other manufacturers did the same, including Magic Chef, Westinghouse, Tappan, and Norge.

Stoves during the 1940s included such features as picture window ovens, oven lights, utensil storage compartments, automatic timers, electric clocks, an outlet plug, warming drawers, and range or condiment sets.

"Speed cooking" and "automatic" were important selling points in the 1940s. For example, a 1947 General Electric advertisement stated "New, Improved Speed Cooking in this Sparkling General Electric Range." This particular stove included a built-in pressure cooker and improved Calrod units for fast, even stove-top heat.

Today old cast-iron and/or porcelain enamel stoves can be found at house sales, auctions, and occasionally at antiques shops and shows. Value is not necessarily determined by age but rather by design, decorative features, and color.

With old cast-iron cooking stoves, it is the nickel-plated trim and colorful ceramic tiles that can make the appliance valuable. On a porcelain-enamel stove, colors and trim colors such as pastel blues and greens create worth.

The demand for these vintage stoves is growing slowly as collectors and admirers seek them out for decorative use in country and Victorian kitchens and restaurants. Some collectors have the preelectric stoves converted for use with electrical power.

As yet there is little demand for the gas and electric stoves manufactured between the 1920s and 1940s. Undoubtedly many of them are still in use today, especially in cottages or cabins that are used as vacation homes. With time and an increased interest in early appliances, these, too, eventually will attract attention.

Toasters

The fireplace of the early nineteenth-century kitchen served as the means of toasting bread. A long-handled toaster would brown the bread over the open fire, or a footed contraption could be set in front of the fire to make toast. These footed or fork-type toasters were used throughout the 1800s.

In 1909 a tin toaster with wire frames to hold the bread in place was patented and named the Knoblock Pyramid Toaster. Bread was toasted by placing the toaster over a burner on the stove.

The year 1909 also saw the advent of the first electric toasters, which were manufactured by General Electric and Westinghouse. The first General Electric D-12 model was a simple porcelain-based unit with wire framing to house the bread against the heating element. The porcelain base not only made this first GE model attractive but it also served as an insulator.

Other GE models made during the following few years had removeable overhead warming trays and decorated porcelain bases. Today these 1909 to 1912

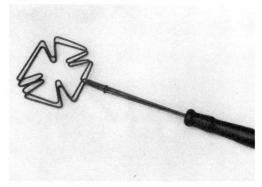

Toaster with black wooden handle, 18″ long, $21.00.

Pyramid toaster, early 1900s, tin with wire frames to hold bread in place, 5″ tall, $10.00.

toasters are quite valuable, costing hundreds of dollars.

Other early toasters were made by Landers, Frary and Clark (the Universal trade name), New Briton, Connecticut; Pacific Electric and Heating, Ontario, California (which later became Hotpoint); Manning Bowman and Company, Simplex Electric Heating, Boston, Massachusetts; Fitzgerald Manufacturing Company, Torrington, Connecticut; Liberty Gauge and Instrument Company, Cleveland, Ohio; Rutenber Electric Company, Marion, Indiana; Bersted Manufacturing Company, Chicago, Illinois; and many others.

The basic principle of operation was similar on most early models. The bread either rested against the hot elements and toasted one side at a time or was held in

Westinghouse electric "Turn-over Toaster, Mansfield, Ohio," late 1920s, 7½" tall, $15.00.

Universal electric toaster by Landers, Frary and Clark, New Britain, Conn., "Pat. Feb. 6, 1906," 6½" tall, $18.00.

Universal electric toaster, late 1920s, 6½" tall, $35.00.

place by a spring-operated frame. The majority of toasters had a warming rack or tray on top. These toasters (sometimes referred to as perchers or pinchers) were manufactured through the 1920s and many are attractive with ornate designs or decorated bases.

Additional advancements and improvements resulted in the manufacture of toasters with turning knobs. These were very popular during the 1920s. For ex-

ample, Westinghouse introduced their first Turnover toaster in 1917; this type of toaster was produced into the 1930s.

The 1924 Montgomery Ward catalog offered an improved electric toaster for $6.95. This toaster "turns toast by automatic door—you do not remove toast from toaster until done. Made of high grade material and nickel-plated."

Collectors also search for the unusual "swing basket" type toasters manufactured during the 1920s. Patented in 1917 by Fred Collier, swing basket toasters were made to swing out to the side and around to turn the toast, or they pulled

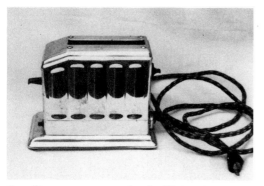

One-slice pop-up toaster by the Waters-Genter Co., early 1930s, "Mpls. Minnesota," $35.00.

Proctor two-slice toaster, "Color Guard, Model 1468C, Proctor Electric Co., Philadelphia," $45.00.

down and swung around. Manning Bowman produced the original swing basket toaster in 1920 and other companies soon followed suit.

The Waters-Genter Company developed an automatic pop-up toaster based on a patent granted to inventor Charles Strite in 1919. The company was selling commercial toasters in 1921 and was purchased by the McGraw Electric Company in 1926. Using Toastmaster as a trade name, McGraw Electric marketed the first automatic pop-up toaster for home use that same year, selling the one-slice toaster for $12.50.

An advertisement in a March 1927 *Saturday Evening Post* proclaimed, "This is National Toaster Month," and went on to describe the new, automatic, Toastmaster: "Three fascinating operations. . . . First you drop a slice of bread into the oven slot. Second, you press down the two levers. This automatically turns on the current and sets the timing device. Third, Pop! Up comes the toast automatically when it's done and the current is automatically turned off. The toast is made in a jiffy because both sides are toasted at the same time." For skeptical readers, the advertisement also stated, "While the Toastmaster is brand new it has been thoroughly tested. For it is a small brother of the big Toastmaster which has been used for many years by famous Restaurants, Hotels, and Sandwich Shops."

By 1934 McGraw Electric Company had introduced a two-slice Toastmaster with an available "hospitality tray," and in 1936 the Chicago Flexible Shaft Company advertised their Sunbeam Silent Automatic Toaster as "silent—no clock mechanism, no ticking. Entirely automatic—has new patented Double Thermostatic Control." This 1936 Sunbeam model sold for $10.95.

Although the early electric toasters were decorative by the very nature of their design, the toasters that were manufactured during the 1930s usually had an embossed or etched design in their chrome sides. By the 1940s toasters were being made in the popular streamlined, modern design with rounded corners and large bulbous shapes such as the 1948 Sunbeam Radiant Control toaster. It was advertised as "Automatic Beyond Belief! All you do is drop in the bread—bread lowers itself automatically . . . toast raises itself silently, without popping or banging."

Early electric toasters are of great interest to collectors, especially examples with unusual decorations, features, or operating mechanisms. Although some are very rare and therefore quite costly (such as the early General Electric with porcelain base), other examples can be found at house sales, auctions, and antiques shops and shows and require only a modest investment. Prices, however, will rise as interest in early electric kitchenware continues to grow.

Waffle Irons

Cast-iron waffle irons were used in America during colonial days when cooking was done at the fireplace. Long, pincer-style handles prevented the cook from burning her hands while the waffles cooked over the open fire.

In the late 1800s, cast-iron waffle irons were made in assorted sizes to fit over the burners on the cookstove. They were made with different designs on the grids, such as stars and hearts, and production of this type continued well into the 1900s.

Several companies manufactured these early models, including Wagner Manufacturing, Sidney, Ohio; Fanner Manufacturing, Cleveland, Ohio; and the Griswold Manufacturing Company, Erie, Pennsylvania.

In the 1800s Griswold Manufacturing produced the "American" design, 8½" waffle iron with the usual grid pattern. After the turn of the century, Griswold

Empress electric waffle iron, manufactured by "Fitzgerald Mfg. Co., Torrington, CT, March 13, 1928 Watts 550, Volts 110," $20.00.

The Empress waffle iron as pictured above, open to show triangular grids.

Griswold Waffle Iron, "American #11, The Griswold Mfg. Co. Erie, Pa., Pat'd Dec. 1, 1908," 6½" across, $85.00.

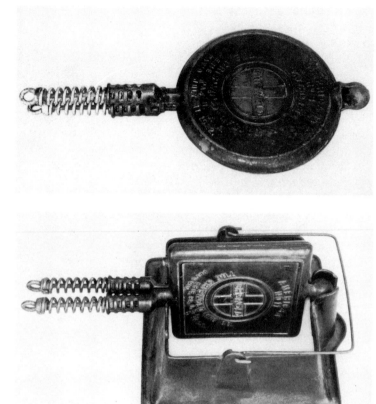

Griswold Waffle Iron, round, "American #8, Pat. No. 161 The Griswold Mfg. Co. Erie, Pa, U.S.A. Pat'd July 11, 1922," 7½" across, $29.00.

The same square Griswold waffle iron pictured previously, closed and ready to turn for complete cooking.

produced numerous other cast-iron models including the Heart and Star waffle iron, which cost $3.85 in 1928. They also produced a square waffle iron in 1927 and a French waffle iron in 1915, which could cook four small round waffles at the same time; and a large waffle iron capable of cooking six waffles at one time. Cast-iron stove-top waffle irons were used well into the 1930s even though electric models were available.

In 1918 an electric waffle iron was manufactured by Landers, Frary and Clark of New Britain, Connecticut; Toastmaster introduced their waffle baker in 1927; and Waters-Genter Company was selling their Waffle Master by 1930.

Over the next decade improvements were made in electric waffle makers, and they were being sold in twin irons, which cooked two waffles at a time (for example, the 1937 Knapp-Monarch Company model that sold for $7.95) and combination waffle iron/sandwich grills that had interchangeable grids.

Electric waffle irons were made by many companies, including National Armstrong Manufacturing Company, Coleman Lamp and Stove Company, General Electric, Majestic Electric Appliance Corporation, Manning Bowman, Sunbeam, and Toastmaster.

During the 1940s waffle irons were square, with streamlined, rounded corners. They were used as both waffle irons and sandwich grills. The 1948 Sunbeam Automatic Waffle Baker had a streamlined design and was advertised as being large enough to serve four people at a time. "Each section of the Sunbeam's famous four-section waffle baker has 20 square inches—more than one-half the size

Waffle iron with decorative ceramic lid (including temperature gauge in the center), marked "Super Electric," manufacturer unknown, $65.00.

of an ordinary round waffle—and the ideal, appetizing size for a single serving."

Early cast-iron waffle makers are highly collectible and desirable for their utilitarian simplicity. Collectors can expect an unusual design, such as a heart-and-star waffle iron or an extra-large restaurant-size waffle iron, to be costly.

Electric waffle makers seem to be attracting some attention, especially unusual examples such as those with decorative ceramic lids, temperature indicators, and intricate art deco designs. As with other electric appliances, this is a growing area of interest for collectors.

Watch for waffle irons to turn up at secondhand stores, yard and house sales, flea markets, and antiques shops and shows.

Electric Mixers

In the early 1900s, development of the small electric motor led to the manufacture of several modest electric gadgets and appliances, one of which was the mixer.

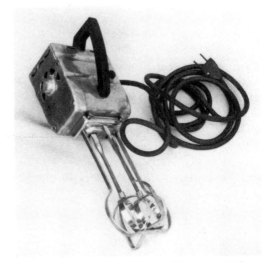

Dormeyer Electric Food Mixer, "Dormeyer Mfg. Co., Chicago, Ill., Pat. 1921, Off/On knob, 110 Volt," $12.00.

Landers, Frary and Clark introduced an electric mixer in 1918, Hobart was selling their KitchenAid stand mixer (through home demonstrations and a female sales force) in 1919, Air-O-Mix Inc. offered an unusual "Whip All" in 1923, and in 1927 the Dormeyer Electric Household Beater was introduced by the MacLeod Manufacturing Company of

39

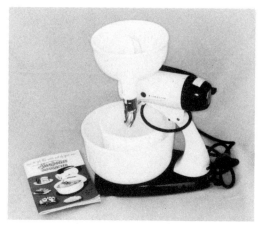

Sunbeam Mixmaster set with original booklet, 1930s, white mixer with black handle and dial, $35.00.

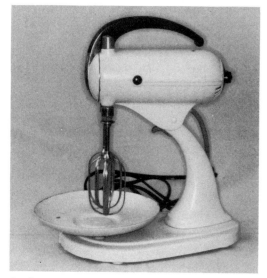

Sunbeam Mixmaster by Chicago Flexible Shaft Co., Chicago, Ill., late 1940s, with ten speeds, $15.00.

Chicago (which became A.F. Dormeyer Manufacturing Company in the 1930s).

In 1930 the Mixmaster by Sunbeam Corporation was introduced and promoted as the appliance of the decade, with a cost of less than $20.00. The Mixmaster remained one of the most popular household appliances through the 1930s and numerous attachments such as a juice extractor, meat grinder, slicer, potato peeler, and chopper could be purchased to use with it.

In 1939 Sunbeam advertised the Mixmaster with Automatic Mix-Finder (a dial to set mixing speed) for $23.75. Additional attachments could be purchased for use with this model, including a slicer-shredder-grater, bean slicer, pea sheller, can opener, colander, coffee grinder, ice cream freezer unit, drink mixer, knife sharpener, and polisher and buffer.

Other companies such as Hamilton Beach, General Electric, and Hobart also were manufacturing mixers through the 1930s and selling them for $18.00 to $30.00. By the 1940s, continued improvements in electric motors led to smaller, sleeker models (the mixers of the 1930s were very large), but it is the crude, early mixers and large electric mixers of the 1930s that collectors are most interested in.

Examples of the very first electric mixers are difficult to find, and collectors should scout antiques shops and shows and check with dealers who specialize in kitchenware and/or electric appliances.

The larger mixers of the 1930s are turning up at antiques shows and flea markets but also still can be found at house sales, estate sales, and auctions.

Coffee Percolators

Prior to the invention of the French Biggin coffeepot in 1800, ground coffee was simply boiled in water and the brew was strained before drinking. The French Biggin conveniently left the coffee grounds in a separate compartment, eliminating the need to strain every cup of coffee. Water would percolate down through the coffee grounds into the coffeepot below.

This type of coffeepot was used throughout the nineteenth century. It was made in various sizes, designs, and materials, including tin, graniteware, copper, and aluminum.

The first electric coffee percolator was

Enamelware coffeepot, black and turquoise, 12″ tall, $35.00.

Small aluminum coffeepot with wooden handle and green glass lid, marked "Pure Aluminum Made in USA," 6″ tall, $12.00.

A 1920 Hotpoint advertisement, featuring the then-popular breakfast sets, complete with coffee percolator, creamer, sugar, and optional waffle iron.

introduced by Landers, Frary and Clark in 1908. The Universal percolator had the advantage of a cold-water pump. This pump allowed the water to begin percolating in just a few minutes instead of the twenty or so minutes it took contemporary electric percolators that were sold by other manufacturers.

Electric percolators were manufac-tured by many different companies, including Dover Manufacturing Company, Knapp-Monarch Company, S.W. Farber Inc., General Electric, Aluminum Goods Manufacturing Company, and others.

Percolator sets and breakfast sets were popular concepts during the 1920s, and many companies marketed their coffee-pots this way. For example, a 1925 advertisement by the Edison Electric Appliance Company for their Hotpoint Breakfast Set stated, "As the breakfast goes, so goes the day. And what could be more auspicious than an electric breakfast of waffles and coffee, prepared in a

Electric coffee percolator with tan Bakelite handles, marked "Continental Silver Co., Inc., 115 Volts, 400 Watts," 13¼" tall, $30.00.

Silex coffee maker with decorative red trim, red tray, and even a red electric cord, late 1930s, $35.00.

jiffy, at the table—with a HOTPOINT Breakfast Set!"

The complete breakfast set included an electric waffle iron, coffee percolator with sugar, creamer, and serving tray; it cost $49.50. The percolator set (percolator, sugar, creamer, and serving tray) cost $35.50.

Glass vacuum-drip coffee makers also became popular during the 1920s after the Silex Company of New York introduced their Silex coffeepot during the 1910s. A 1914 trade advertisement illustrated the origin of the Silex name by describing the coffeepot as "**S**anitary and **I**nteresting method of making **L**uscious Coffee. It is **E**asy to operate on account of its being **X**ray transparent."

Old coffeepots are a desirable addition to a collection of kitchenware and also are categorically collected by those who search for graniteware, copper, tin, and so forth.

Electric coffeepots are not as eagerly sought after yet; however, this will change with the ever-growing interest in early electric appliances. Look for examples with etched art deco designs or unusual lines and coffeepots that were made to complement a particular line of dinnerware.

Other Electric Appliances

The early 1900s through the 1940s was a period of prolific growth in the development of new electric appliances and gadgets due to the widespread availability of electric power in most homes and the continued advances of domestic engineering. Manufacturers looked to almost every kitchenware item for a potential new electric product to patent and market. As a result, numerous other electric kitchen servants were being sold, but they were not always as convenient or practical as the simple, manual gadget. For example, items such as the electric flour sifter, electric spatula, electric egg cooker, and electric coffee grinder appeared on the market and virtually disappeared just as quickly (or became specialty items).

Capital sandwich grill with temperature gauge in lid, circa 1930s, manufacturer unknown, $35.00.

Early electric flour sifter with original box, Miracle Electric Co., Chicago, Ill., 8″ tall, $35.00.

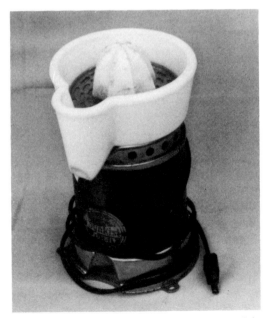

"Sunkist Juicit, Chicago Electric Mfg. Co., Model 19," 9″ tall, $4.75.

"Mixall Mixes Drinks—Whips, Etc. 110–120 Volts AC 75 Watts. Oil in oil holes only. Chronmaster Electric Corp., New York, Chicago, Patent Claims Allowed," on/off switch, mixer raises up so glass may be removed, 12″ tall, $20.00.

Electric juicers were being sold by the late 1920s; the Sunkist Jr. model by A.C. Gilbert Company of New Haven, Connecticut, sold for $14.95. These electric gadgets continued to be made through the 1940s (and are available today) but never became a huge success.

Westinghouse introduced an electric frying pan in 1911 (which also could be turned upside down and used as a hot plate), but electric frying pans did not become popular until the 1950s.

Armstrong's Standard Stamping Company of Marysville, Ohio, introduced an electric broiler in 1916, but it was 1930 before tabletop broilers achieved any popularity.

Electric blenders were sold by the 1920s after the Arnold Electric Company of Racine, Wisconsin, began producing them. However, they mainly were used on a commercial basis by restaurants and other establishments for mixing drinks.

Early electric broiler, black Bakelite handles, "Broil Maid Chromium on solid brass, Guaranteed Rustless, Forman Family Inc., Brooklyn, N.Y.," 12" across, $20.00.

Hobart's KitchenAid coffee grinder, circa 1937, $30.00.

Early electric hot plate, manufacturer unknown, $20.00.

After the John Oster Manufacturing Company began making blenders in the 1930s, they also were used for pureeing fruits and vegetables and were promoted as a household item that was convenient for cooking as well as for mixing drinks. By the 1940s several companies were making blenders, and improvements and added features made them a popular kitchenware item.

Unusual electric appliances or gadgets can be found almost anywhere. Collectors find they turn up at house and yard sales, secondhand stores, auctions, and antiques shops and shows. Prices are very reasonable—for the time being—but expect prices to increase as collectors find merit in early electric appliances. This especially will hold for those examples that achieved only limited success and, therefore, had small production numbers.

44

CHAPTER 3 Cookware

Cookware has evolved over the years from the black iron kettle simmering over an open fire to the high-tech plastic used in the microwave and the copper-bottomed stainless steel pots and pans placed on top of the stove. In between, various materials have been used to make the jobs of cooking and cleanup less tedious, and collectors are interested in each of them.

The iron and copper cookware of the 1700s is scarce but these same materials were used well into the nineteenth century, and examples from the Victorian era still can be found today. The plain, useful tinware pieces and colorful graniteware are very popular collectibles. Graniteware is often a specialty item for collectors. Because several companies manufactured this cookware, a variety of objects were made in a wide array of colors.

Early glass cookware and oven-to-table lines are receiving attention as collectors search for new areas to explore.

Today, even in the most modern kitchen, iron and copper cookware hanging by the stove or an assortment of graniteware stacked on a shelf blends the old effectively with the new.

Iron Cookware

Iron has been used to produce cookware in America since the early seventeenth century. Wrought-iron (iron pieces hammered into shape at a forge) cookware includes skewers, trivets, and grills. Early cast-iron cookware (made by pouring hot metal into molds) includes the pots and kettles that were used for cooking over the fire. Ironware, whether wrought or cast, was very plain in design and was created strictly for function.

Cast iron remained popular through the 1800s and the advent of the coal-/woodburning stove created a need for additional cookware pieces. As a result, assorted pots, frying pans, muffin and cornbread pans, and teakettles were made.

Collectors will find the majority of nineteenth-century iron cookware has no markings. With few exceptions, early pieces have no names or dates to identify

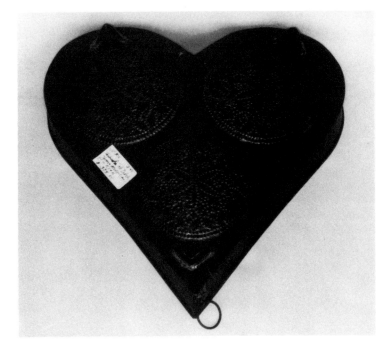

Unusual Pennsylvania Dutch cheese mold with punch-tin design, 12″ across, $375.00.

Iron frying pan for fireplace
cooking, 11″ wide, $45.00.

Hand-forged iron oven ash retriever, 11½″ wide,
$75.00.

Small iron pot for fireplace cooking, 8″ wide by
5½″ high, $35.00.

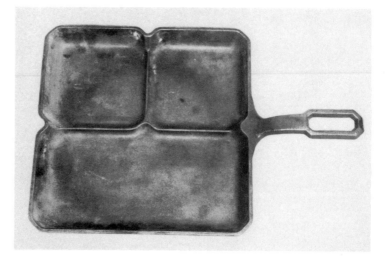

Griswold iron skillet, "Colonial
Breakfast Skillet, Griswold,
Erie, PA, USA, Pat. Applied For
666," 9″ across, $39.00.

48

Iron and enamelware egg poacher, 9½″ wide, $48.00.

Griswold Dutch oven "Tite-Top, No. 7," 9″ wide by 4½″ deep, $69.00.

metalsmiths. Any ironware with a marking has a value a great deal higher than an unmarked example.

Factory-made cast-iron cookware remained popular during the early 1900s. The 1924 Montgomery Ward catalog offered cast-iron skillets in three sizes (10¼″, 11¼″, and 12½″) for $0.89 to $1.69. They also offered a Griswold 8-quart cast-iron Safety Kettle, "to be used for all kinds of cooking or stewing," for $2.69. A Danish apple cake pan with seven cups sold for $0.98.

The Griswold Manufacturing Com-

Griswold cast-iron skillet #3, "Griswold, Erie, PA, USA, 7 09 A," 6½" across, $25.00.

Griswold cast-iron popover pan, $35.00.

Tea-size "Krusty Korn Kobs, Reg. in US Pat. Off., Wagner Ware, Sidney, Ohio #459 Pat'd July 6, 1920," 7½" long, $55.00.

pany of Erie, Pennsylvania, produced high-quality cast-iron cookware from the 1880s until the 1950s. Named after Matthew Griswold (after Griswold bought out earlier partners), the company grew and expanded to include cookware for restaurants, a line of cast-aluminum cookware, small electric appliances, and chrome- or porcelain-finished cookware. It was, however, the cast-iron line of kitchenware that remained the mainstay of the company. Griswold produced cast-iron skillets, griddles, waffle irons, fryers, Dutch ovens, muffin pans, breadstick pans, saucepans, and breakfast skillets.

Look for ironware pieces to turn up at house sales, flea markets, antiques shops and shows, and auctions. Ironware is functional as well as collectible and while most pieces are not expensive, a rare or unusual example, such as an advertising piece, candy or cake mold, or a late nineteenth-century skillet will be quite costly.

Copper Cookware

Like iron, copper has been used for cookware for centuries. A soft ore, copper is an excellent heat conductor. During colonial days copper was hand wrought to make kettles and pans that were lined with tin. These early copper pieces were probably made from the ore mined in Connecticut. Copper was later found in Pennsylvania and the nearby Great Lakes region.

Although copper cookware was difficult to keep clean and needed routine repair to keep the tin lining intact, it remained popular through the 1800s because it was lighter than iron cookware. During the Victorian era copper was found mainly in the kitchens of the upper-class, because it was quite expensive.

An assortment of cookware and utensils was available during the nineteenth century, including saucepans, stock pots, frying pans, baking sheets, molds, coffeepots and teapots, and measuring cups.

Although examples of copper cookware from the eighteenth century can only

Copper gooseneck teakettle, 7″ tall by 7″ wide, $195.00.

Copper mold, 5″ wide, $12.00.

Copper scoop, 7″ long, $22.50.

be found on display in museums, collectors still can find examples from the late 1800s. Look for copper cookware at antiques shops and shows and particularly from dealers who specialize in old kitchenware.

Tinware

The early nineteenth century saw the development of a tin-plated iron called tinware. Sheets of iron were made thin by putting them through a roller. The next step was to dip the thin metal sheet into hot tin, giving it a shiny coating.

Ornate copper and silver teapot, 7½″ tall, $89.00.

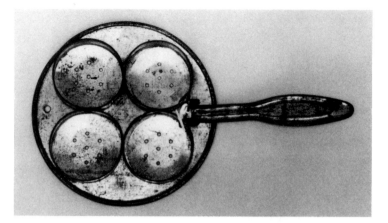

Tin egg poacher, 6½" wide, $25.00.

Tin mold with six hearts, each heart 3", $75.00.

Tin rice ball, 4½" across, $35.00.

By the 1840s tinsmith shops could be found all over the country. From large sheets of tin, tinsmiths produced such items as pots and pans, coffeepots and teapots, pie plates, fish kettles, frying pans, bread pans, and boilers. An assortment of smaller cooking utensils such as cookie cutters was made from the scrap metal.

Tin peddlers traveled throughout rural areas selling tinware goods from the back of horse-drawn wagons. Barges moving down the Mississippi River became floating emporiums of tin goods. By the late 1800s tinware also could be ordered from mail-order catalogs.

This lightweight, shiny metal was easy to maintain, but was usually very plain. Some pieces were decorated with designs made by punching, scalloping, or piercing the tin. This was first done by hand and then later by machine.

In Pennsylvania the Dutch were recognized for their attractive punched tinware. This method of decorating cookware extended to include the punch-tin pie safes that are eagerly sought by antiques enthusiasts today.

While sales of tin pots and pans fell off with the introduction of the more-popular graniteware and aluminum, items such as cookie cutters, cookie sheets, and especially baking sets remained popular through the years and continued to be sold into the early twentieth century. For example, the 1924 Montgomery Ward catalog advertised the tin VanDeusen cake

Tin cheese molds, 4″ across, $6.00 each.

Muffin tin, "George Urban Milling Co. Buffalo, N.Y.," 10½″ long by 8″ wide, $14.00.

Factory-made pie tin, "New England Flaky Crust Pie, 10¢ deposit, Table Talk," 9″, $12.00.

Kreamer, 8″ cake pan, $8.00.

Tin mold, decorative strawberry design, 6″ long, $23.00.

baking set, which included one round tubed loaf mold, two layer molds, an egg whip, measuring cup, and recipe book for $1.29. Large tin cookie sheets could be purchased for $0.42 each.

Graniteware

The same thin sheets of ironware that were coated with melted tin were also coated with enamel in the late 1800s, resulting in the popular cookware called graniteware.

Graniteware was affordable, easy to clean, and colorful. No longer restricted to the blacks and grays of iron and tin,

Graniteware pie plate, black
with white speckles, 9″, $3.00.

White graniteware colander
with blue trim, 10½″ across,
bought at auction for $2.00.

housewives and cooks enjoyed the wide
array of graniteware colors.

Graniteware was first introduced at
the 1876 Philadelphia Centennial Expo-
sition and was soon being manufactured
by several companies. Lalance and Grosjean Manufacturing Company marketed
the popular agateware, which was advertised as being very safe to use because
it contained no arsenic or lead in the
spotted enamel coating. Lalance and
Grosjean identified their wares first by
burning "L&G" into their product and
then later by attaching a blue paper label
to their goods.

Other companies that produced

Enameled teakettle, tan with chrome lid and
Bakelite on handle, 10″ tall, $35.00.

54

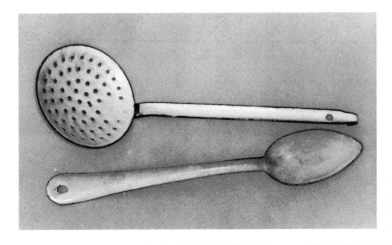

White graniteware spoon, 13½″ long, $1.00. Ladle, 13½″ long, $2.50. Both were lucky garage sale finds.

Graniteware pudding pan, blue with white swirls, 8″ wide by 3″ high, $25.00.

French enamelware eggcup with unusual design, 2¼″ tall, $125.00.

graniteware included the St. Louis Stamping Company, St. Louis, Missouri; the Iron Clad Manufacturing Company, New York City; the Lisk Manufacturing Company, National Enameling and Stamping Company, and Republic Stamping and Enameling Company—all from Ohio. Most of these companies also used a paper label to identify their products.

The many different cookware items made of graniteware included coffeepots and teapots, saucepans, pots, preserving kettles, boilers, griddles, colanders, and muffin pans. These items were made in several speckled colors including red, yellow, robin's egg blue, cobalt blue, brown, green, gray, and black.

After 1900 changes were made in the manufacture of graniteware. Sheet iron was no longer used as a base metal as manufacturers turned to steel. New colors

Unusual light blue graniteware teapot with floral decoration, 10½″ tall, $145.00.

Graniteware frying pan, blue
with white speckles, 8", $18.00.

Child's mug, blue with white swirl, 3" tall, $15.00.

Unusual French gravy dish and lid (7" tall by 4"
wide) that allows the gravy to be poured with or
without the fat, depending on which opening is
turned to the spout, white enamelware, $65.00.

were introduced and various designs were
produced. Some graniteware was made
a solid white with colored trim while other
pieces were speckled, marbleized, and
streaked.

A 1910 Montgomery Ward and Company *Groceries Price List* catalog advertised a fourteen-piece enamel kitchen
outfit for $1.98. The catalog stated that
it consisted of "a fine assortment of necessary kitchen utensils . . . each piece
heavily enameled (two coats) with a pretty
light brown and white mottled surface
and warranted free from imperfections."
The set included wash basin, pudding pan,
1-quart cup, two pie plates, Berlin kettle
with cover, dipper, basting spoon, preserving kettle, saucepan, teakettle, colander, perforated soup ladle, and coffeepot.

Some collectors today look for rare
green, black, pink, brown, red, lavender,
and yellow graniteware; these pieces
command top price. Other collectors are
happy building a collection of the more
common blue, gray, and white graniteware pieces that are still readily available.

Graniteware remained popular
through the 1920s and then most companies closed down during the Depression. Because graniteware has again been
manufactured since the 1950s, collectors
should study examples carefully. Older

56

pieces will show signs of use and rust—graniteware is somewhat fragile and constant use will wear the enamel off in spots. By the late 1920s the popularity of graniteware gave way to a new cookware—aluminum.

Aluminum Cookware

Although aluminum cookware was first introduced in the United States in 1892, it was costly and inferior to the popular tinware and graniteware widely being used. As a result, aluminum cookware was not popular until the 1920s. By then, manufacturers greatly had improved their product and brought the cost down to make it a competitive cookware.

The 1918 Montgomery Ward *Summer Sale Book* featured a page devoted to their "Big Royal Aluminum Sale." A Royal teakettle could be purchased for $1.89; a Royal aluminum saucepan set (three pans) cost $1.45; Royal bread and cake pans were $0.37 each; and the "Choice Ten-Piece Royal Aluminum Set" including

kettle, three pans, two pie plates, dipper, measuring cup, and salt and pepper was priced at $3.74.

Several companies manufactured aluminum cookware in the early 1900s, including the Aluminum Cooking Utensil Company, New Kensington, Pennsylvania, which advertised their Wear-Ever line of aluminum products. A 1911 advertisement for Wear-Ever stated, "No! They are not all the same. Wear-Ever Aluminum Utensils are different." The advertisement went on to explain the purity, thickness, finish, and handles of these products.

Another successful manufacturer of aluminum cookware was the Wagner Manufacturing Company, Sidney, Ohio. In 1922 an advertisement for the Wagner Cast Aluminum Ware line of teakettles said, "The tea kettle is the heart of your kitchen equipment. . . . After using a Wagner kettle for twenty years as many others have done, you'll agree that Wagner makes the finest cooking utensils in the world." The Wagner teapots included the Sidney, Grand Prize, and Priscilla.

The Aluminum Goods Manufactur-

Griswold aluminum teakettle, "5 quart Colonial Design Cast Aluminum Erie, PA, USA Pat. Sept. 9, 1913," $20.00.

Griswold #5 cast aluminum
frying pan with lid, 7" wide,
$85.00.

A 1936 advertisement for the modern-looking
Mirro aluminum ware.

ing Company, Manitowic, Wisconsin,
produced popular lines of aluminum ware
known as Viko and Mirro during the 1920s
and 1930s. A 1936 advertisement for Mirro,
"The Finest Aluminum," offered several
items of "unusual beauty and smart styl-
ing," such as a 2-quart sauce pan for $0.59,
a mixing bowl with lip and grip for $1.00,
and a 4-quart whistling teakettle for $1.98.

By the 1920s aluminum cookware included items such as kettles, pots and
pans, double boilers, strainers, roasters,
cake pans, pudding pans, casseroles, and
muffin pans.

In 1938 copper-bottomed stainless
steel Revere Ware by Revere Copper and
Brass, Inc., Rome, New York, was introduced. The stainless steel Revere Ware
was an immediate success, and although
aluminum remained popular for some
time, Revere Ware was strong competition.

Examples of early aluminum ware
can be found at secondhand shops, flea
markets, house sales, and some antiques
shops. It can be had for very little cost.

Glass Cookware

Corning Glass Works, Corning, New York,
introduced Pyrex Ovenware in 1915. In
an advertisement in the May 1919 issue

Fire-King pie plate, blue, 8″, $8.00.

Set of four Fire-King custard cups, blue, 1¾″ tall by 3¼″ wide, the set is $15.00.

Blue Fire-King casserole with lid, 8″ wide by 3″ high, $48.00.

of the *Ladies' Home Journal,* Corning said, "Perfect Baking requires thorough, uniform heat . . . because glass lets in the heat which metal keeps out, Pyrex bakes better, and at much lower temperatures." The advertisement also told readers that using Pyrex would conserve fuel and retain food flavors.

Corning's glass casserole dishes, custard cups, and pie plates maintained steady sales through the 1930s when the Pyrex Top-of-the-Stove glass cookware was introduced in 1936. Then Corning could offer double boilers, saucepans, skillets, coffee makers, and percolators.

The May 1936 *Good Housekeeping* magazine included an advertisement for Pyrex Top-of-the-Stove Ware that said, "It's the latest miracle in glass. . . . A new Pyrex Saucepan that will withstand the heat of the open flame!" The advantages of the new cookware included a removable handle and standard covers that fit both the ovenware and top-of-the-stove pieces. Furthermore, it saved fuel, it was nonporous, and it always looked new. You could also watch the food cook.

In 1937 a Pyrex three-piece set with two saucepans and a skillet (with removable chrome handles) cost $2.65.

Anchor Hocking Glass Corporation, Lancaster, Ohio, introduced their Fire-King line of ovenware in 1941. This was manufactured in crystal (clear glass) and sapphire blue until the 1950s.

The H.C. Fry Glass Company, Rochester, Pennsylvania, also produced ovenware during the 1920s and 1930s. This ovenware was produced in an opalescent white, referred to as pearl, and in various colors.

Glass cookware can be found at house and yard sales, auctions, secondhand shops, and antiques shops and shows. Blue Fire-King and Pearl Fry Glass are more desirable pieces among collectors than the crystal Pyrex.

CHAPTER 4 Everyday
Dinnerware

The past few decades have seen a renewed interest in early everyday tableware, which has left boxes and attics to take up residence in the kitchen cabinet once again. Collectors study the various patterns, styles, colors, and objects that were manufactured as well as the companies that produced these attractive place settings and novelty pieces popular from 1900 through the 1940s.

Carnival glass was made for the middle class who admired, but could not afford, the turn-of-the-century art glass made by such men as Louis Comfort Tiffany. Then when styles began to change and the popularity of carnival glass waned, manufacturers turned their attention to the more profitable depression glass that could be cheaply mass produced.

The popular geometric shapes of the art deco period influenced the pattern of the colorful Fiesta Ware manufactured by Homer Laughlin China Company. Collectors are finding there is great demand for tableware made from the 1930s through the 1970s.

Any particular type of dinnerware can be a specialty area for collectors. Glassware and pottery organizations, collectors' associations, glassware shows, and pottery shows are increasing and are evidence of the ever-growing interest in this area of collecting.

Carnival Glass

Carnival glass is iridized pressed glass that was mass produced during the early 1900s. The process of iridizing the glass involved the use of sprayed-on metal salts to give the mold color. The glass was then reheated to give it a shiny look.

This popular iridized glass was first produced in 1907 by the Fenton Art Glass Company of West Virginia. Frank Fenton originally established his company in Ohio in 1905 and built the factory in Williamstown, West Virginia, the following year.

Another company responsible for producing large quantities of carnival glass was the Northwood Glass Company, Wheeling, West Virginia. Founded by Harry Northwood in 1902, this company is credited with developing many of the popular colors used in the manufacture of carnival glass and had twenty-one years of successful production prior to closing in 1923 after Harry Northwood died.

A third company, the Imperial Glass Company, was producing carnival glass by 1910. This company was started in Bellaire, Ohio, in 1901 and produced several popular glasswares over the years. During the 1930s the company became known as Imperial Glass Corporation and produced much depression glass.

Other companies that manufactured

Depression glass cup and saucer, Doric and Pansy pattern, ultramarine, $19.00.

Carnival glass dish, purple, grapes and leaves decoration, 7″, $65.00.

Carnival glass dish with fluted edges, purple, 7″, $25.00.

carnival glass include Cambridge Glass Company, Cambridge, Ohio; Heisey Glass Company, Newark, Ohio; Indiana Glass Company, Dunkirk, Indiana; Jenkins Glass Company, Kokomo, Indiana; Millersburg Glass Company, Millersburg, Ohio; and Westmoreland Glass Company, Pennsylvania.

These companies and others created iridized pressed glass in more than 1,000 patterns and styles. The various colors were achieved by tinting either the base glass or the iridescent spray in dark or pastel shades. Dark colors include green, blue, red, and amethyst, and pastel colors are found in shades of peach, green, blue, aqua, smoke, and white.

Carnival glass remained popular through the 1920s. This inexpensive glassware could be purchased at the local emporium, from department stores, and through mail-order catalogs. It was not, however, sold as "carnival" glass. Manufacturers gave their product different names such as Taffeta Lustre, which was sold by the Northwood Glass Company.

When the sale of iridized glass dropped off in the 1920s, large amounts of inventory still filled the warehouses. Carnivals, circuses, and movie theaters purchased the stock very cheaply and used it as game prizes and free gifts. As a result, the name carnival glass was generically assigned to the once-popular glassware of the early 1900s.

The last twenty years have seen a renewed interest in carnival glass as collectors discover the beauty of the numerous colors and patterns and learn about the companies associated with the manufacture of iridized glassware.

Dinnerware, serving pieces, novelty

Marigold pitcher with four glasses, pitcher 9″ tall, glasses 6″ tall, the set is $59.00.

Carnival glass grape bowl, marigold, 9″, $48.00.

items and small whimseys are all highly collectible. Color, pattern, object, and manufacturer influence pricing. A complete collection of dinnerware still can be had for a small investment, if a collector is interested in one of the more abundant colors, such as marigold.

Depression Glass

Depression glass is the name given to the inexpensive, machine-molded glassware that was mass produced during the 1920s, 1930s, and 1940s. This colorful glassware sold at five-and-ten-cent stores, hardware stores, and through mail-order catalogs; it also was used as a product premium by many companies. For example, a small 1936 American Seed Company advertisement in a national women's magazine told readers a "32-piece Rose-Pink Glassware Dinner Set given for easy selling of our fine vegetable and flower seeds at 10¢ a pack."

Depression glass was manufactured by many companies including the Federal Glass Company, Columbus, Ohio; Hazel-Atlas Glass Company, Clarksville, West Virginia; Hocking Glass Company, Lancaster, Ohio; Indiana Glass Company, Dunkirk, Indiana; Jeannette Glass Company, Jeannette, Pennsylvania;

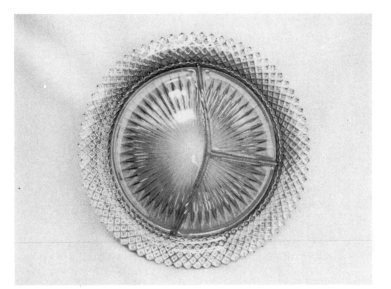

Depression glass grill plate, pink, Miss America pattern, 10¼″, $17.50.

Salt and pepper, green, cloverleaf pattern, $27.50.

Platter, blue, Royal Lace pattern, 13″, $50.00.

MacBeth-Evans Glass Company, Charleroi, Pennsylvania; Duncan and Miller Glass Company, Washington, Pennsylvania; Libbey Glass Company, Toledo, Ohio; Paden City Glass Company, Paden City, West Virginia; and U.S. Glass Company, which had several factories in Pennsylvania.

Altogether these companies manufactured and sold depression glass in more than ninety different patterns and more than twenty-five colors. The colors are classified as transparent (which includes pink, green, and amber), translucent (which includes the colorless glass known as crystal), and opaque (which has a milky appearance such as the green jadite).

Various styles emerged during the years depression glass was produced. For example, early dinnerware, luncheon sets, and glasses were decorated with popular lace patterns such as Adam, issued from 1932 to 1934 by the Jeannette Glass Company. Adam was available in pink, green, crystal, yellow, and limited delphite blue.

Along with patterns of lace, those patterns with flowers and birds were very popular by the mid-1930s. Mayfair, a pattern depicting roses and arches, was produced by the Federal Glass Company. This pattern was available in green, amber, and crystal. Another flowery pattern, Sharon, or Cabbage Rose, was also issued by Federal Glass from 1935 to 1939 and

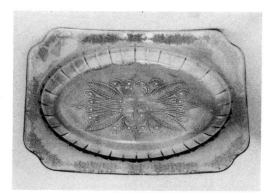

Platter, green, Adam pattern, 12″, $17.00.

Moderntone dinner plate, cobalt, 9″, $13.50.

was available in pink, green, amber, and limited crystal.

Art deco influence can be seen in the geometric designs of a depression glass pattern such as Moderntone, which was produced by the Hazel-Atlas Glass Company from 1934 to 1942 and was reissued during the 1950s. Moderntone was manufactured in amethyst, blue, and opaque.

Fancy depression glass, reminiscent of nineteenth-century cut glass, was also popular during the 1930s. Rock Crystal issued by McKee Glass Company was an imitation cut-glass pattern available in crystal, frosted crystal, crystal with gold decorations, and a number of other colors.

Opaque depression glass is a very specific area of interest for many collectors. Several popular patterns were made of the milky glass, including Laurel is-

sued by McKee Glass Company in the 1930s. This tableware was made in French ivory, jade green, white opal, and soudre blue. A line of kitchenware items including canisters and salt and peppers was available in this pattern, too.

Collectors of depression glass are interested in color, pattern, the object itself, and the manufacturer, but usually collect according to color and pattern. Rarity, whether in color, pattern, or object, will have an effect on pricing but collectors still can build extensive collections of depression glass. Collectors should study their areas of interest because many patterns have been reissued during the last several years.

Depression glass can be found at antiques shops and shows, house and yard sales, auctions, flea markets, and glassware shows. Prices can be quite reasonable for patterns and colors still in good supply, such as Federal Glass Company's Heritage pattern in crystal, Hocking Glass Company's Block Optic pattern in pink, and MacBeth-Evans Glass Company's Petalware in pink or crystal.

Fiesta Ware

Fiesta ware, a colorful and modernistic tableware, was produced by the Homer Laughlin China Company of Newell, West Virginia.

The American public was introduced to this art deco dinnerware at the 1936 Pottery and Glass Show in Pittsburgh, Pennsylvania, and it became an immediate success.

An Englishman named Frederick Rhead is recognized as having created the Fiesta pattern (a band of rings, graduating in width) for the Homer Laughlin China Company.

When first produced in 1936, Fiesta ware was available in the original colors of yellow, green, ivory, cobalt, and red. A turquoise was added in 1938. Of the

Fiesta ware grill plate, yellow, 10″, $20.00.

Fiesta cup and saucer, yellow, cup is 2½″ tall by 3½″ wide, saucer is 6½″, $16.00.

Fiesta chop plate, navy blue, 12″, $30.00.

original Fiesta ware colors, red is quite scarce and the most expensive to collect. Red Fiesta ware was made with uranium oxide and during World War II, the government requested that the Homer Laughlin China Company cease any production involving the use of this material. As a result, no red Fiesta ware was produced for several years.

During the 1950s the original colors of green, cobalt, and ivory were discon-tinued and replaced with the "fifties" colors of gray, rose, dark green, char-treuse, and a medium green issued in 1959. Production continued through the 1960s. Fiesta was redesigned in 1969 and sold in mango red, antique gold, and turf green. Production of Fiesta ware ceased in 1973.

The colors of the 1950s were not as popular with the public as the original six, therefore, not as much Fiesta ware was produced in those colors. Collectors

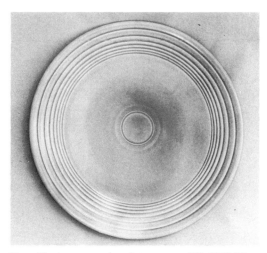

Rare Fiesta ware cake plate, green, 10″, $250.00.

Cup, Carnival pattern that at one time was given away in Quaker Oatmeal boxes, green, 3½″ tall, $1.00.

Harlequin gravy boat, orange, 3½″ tall by 7″ wide, $17.50.

find that those colors, like the red Fiesta, are more expensive.

Fiesta ware is easily identified by its marking. *Fiesta* is usually indented or stamped in ink on the bottom of the piece. There are, however, a few exceptions: teacups, juice tumblers, and salt and peppers had no markings.

In 1987 Homer Laughlin China Company reissued Fiesta ware in five new "eighties" colors: pink, blue, apricot, white, and black. This new Fiesta is both dishwasher and microwave safe and is already being collected now for the future.

The Homer Laughlin China Company also produced other lines that were similar to Fiesta, but were less expensive and were limited in production. These included Harlequin and Riviera ware.

HARLEQUIN

Harlequin was manufactured during the years 1938 to 1964 and was sold exclusively by F.W. Woolworth stores. This line of tableware was lighter and thinner than Fiesta ware, but the design was very similar. Harlequin was made in many of the same colors as Fiesta, along with a spruce green and maroon.

Harlequin was reissued and sold through F.W. Woolworth once again in 1979. At that time it was available in turquoise, green, yellow, and coral. The early 1980s saw this pattern again reissued.

Harlequin can be distinguished from Fiesta because it has no markings (Fiesta ware is marked). If the pattern is examined closely, you will notice that the outermost ring on Harlequin pieces is farther from the rim than it is on Fiesta ware.

Harlequin plate, yellow, 7″, $5.00.

Riviera mugs, green and yellow, 4″ tall by 3½″ wide, each $50.00.

RIVIERA WARE

Riviera ware was another less-expensive tableware manufactured by the Homer Laughlin China Company. This unmarked line sold through the Murphy Company and was easily recognizable with its square plates and cup handles. Riviera ware was made from 1938 to 1950 and sold in mauve blue, red, yellow, light green, ivory, and a limited dark blue.

The Homer Laughlin China Company produced other popular patterned dinnerwares including Blue Medallion, Carnation Beauty, Flying Bluebird, Gold and Cobalt, Gold Lace, Pink Moss Rose, Pink Rose, Pink Rose and Daisy, Rose and Lattice, Violet Spray, and White and Green Persian; all were produced during the 1920s and often decorated with decals.

Along with Fiesta, Harlequin, and Riviera ware, the 1930s and 1940s saw other popular dinnerware lines produced such as Hacienda, Briar Rose, Serenade, Tango, English Garden, Blue Willow, and Rhythm.

Hall China

The Hall China Company has produced an assortment of tableware that is sought after by collectors today. Known for their prolific manufacture of teapots, this company began in East Liverpool, Ohio, in 1903. Along with teapots, Hall produced assorted dinnerware lines that have grown increasingly popular.

One particular area of interest for collectors is the Autumn Leaf dinnerware/tableware pattern. Autumn Leaf was produced during the period from 1933 to 1977 specifically for the Jewel Tea Company. This grocery store chain used Autumn Leaf (dinnerware, glasses, stemware, and kitchenware) as premiums.

Other companies produced the Autumn Leaf pattern, including Paden City Pottery Company, Crooksville China Company, and Harker Pottery Company,

Autumn Leaf cup and saucer, cup is 2½″ tall by 3″ wide, saucer is 6″, $20.00.

Hall's Autumn Leaf teapot, 7-cup size, $45.00.

Autumn Leaf bowl, 7", $15.00.

so collectors must check for Hall markings.

Other popular dinnerware produced by Hall China Company includes Crocus (also referred to as Holland), which was made in the 1930s and used as a premium by Best Tea; Poppy (also called Orange Poppy), which was made from the 1930s through the 1950s and was used as a pre-mium by the Great American Tea Company; Red Poppy also was produced be-tween the 1930s and 1950s for use by the Grand Union Tea Company; Taverne was a popular pattern produced during the 1930s and used as a premium by several different companies; and Tulip, which was made from the 1930s through the 1950s.

Collectors will find Hall China at

Hall's Autumn Leaf dessert plates, 6″, each $1.50.

Blue Ridge platter, decorated with flowers, 12″, $15.00.

house and yard sales, flea markets, antiques shops and shows, and auctions. Even the popular Autumn Leaf pattern still is readily available for collecting and prices remain reasonable.

Southern Potteries, Inc.

Southern Potteries, Inc., established in 1917 in Erwin, Tennessee, produced popular dinnerware lines in numerous patterns until they closed in 1957.

During the early years of production their wares were decorated with either

Small Blue Ridge plate, floral design, 6″, $4.00.

Blue Ridge plate, hand-decorated with flowers, 9″, $7.00.

Blue Ridge plate, fluted edges with floral design, 10″, $4.00.

decals or hand-painted designs. By the 1930s the hand-decorated, underglazed lines were becoming so popular that Blue Ridge became the trade name for these pieces.

Blue Ridge dinnerware was made in several shapes and decorated in hundreds of patterns, depicting flowers, fruit, French peasants, barnyard animals, and trees.

Some of Southern Potteries' earliest hand-decorated patterns date from the 1920s and include Moss Rose, Eventide,

Luna, Ming Tree, Mountain Cherry, Quilted Fruit, Rooster, Southern Dogwood, Tropical, Tulips, and Weathervane.

Later patterns include Crab Apple, which was produced during the 1930s and 1940s, and Autumn Apple, Cock O' the Walk, Mardi Gras, and Rend Leaf, which were all produced during the 1940s.

Some of the Blue Ridge dinnerware decorated during the 1940s was signed by the artist and these pieces are prized by collectors.

Collectors should look for Blue Ridge pieces in excellent condition and avoid those pieces with chips or crazing. Blue Ridge is very affordable, with the exception of those shapes that have become hard to find, such as Trellis and Monticello.

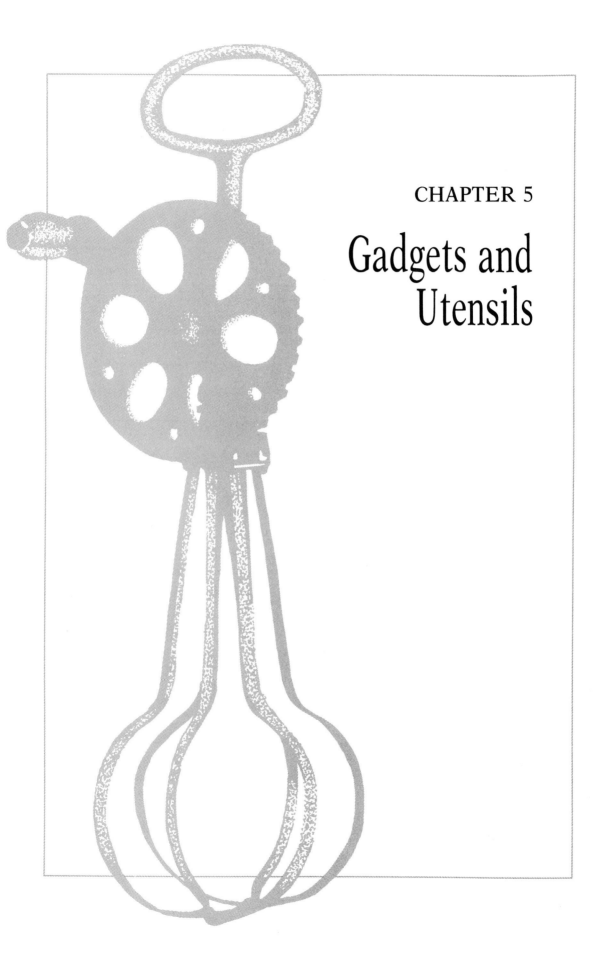

CHAPTER 5

Gadgets and Utensils

For the collector interested in old kitchenware items, gadgets and utensils offer wide-range diversity. Gagdets are usually small mechanical devices, and utensils are other tools or containers used in the kitchen. Many gadgets and utensils are centuries old while others were developed as recently as the nineteenth-century Industrial Revolution.

The wooden or iron "primitive" kitchenwares of the eighteenth and nineteenth centuries were strictly utilitarian and often very crude. Wooden gadgets and utensils were hand-crafted at home, while the local smith provided the iron necessities.

With the advent of the Industrial Revolution many household items were invented, patented, and mass produced. For the most part these Victorian era kitchen tools were made of metal, were convenient to use, and were easy to clean.

After the turn of the century, the stark, sterile kitchen, which was popular during the late 1800s, began to change as industry, modernization, and the influ-ence of color brought about numerous changes. By the 1920s color could be found in flooring, wall treatments, appliances, furniture, cookware, and kitchen tools. First metal and then stainless steel kitchenware was made with colored wooden handles until plastic was introduced in the late 1940s. White, black, green, red, blue, and yellow were the most popular colors found on gadgets and utensils.

The old kitchen tools collectors find today were manufactured by many companies, including Acme Metal Goods Manufacturing Company, Newark, New Jersey; Bromwell Wire Goods, Cincinnati, Ohio; A&J Manufacturing Company, Binghamton, New York; Aluminum Goods Manufacturing Company, Two Rivers, Wisconsin; Dazey Churn and Manufacturing Company, St. Louis, Missouri; Ekco Housewares Company, Chicago, Illinois; Landers, Frary and Clark, New Britain, Connecticut; Fred J. Meyers Manufacturing Company, Hamilton, Ohio; National Enameling and Stamping Company, Milwaukee, Wisconsin; Rival Manufacturing Company, Kansas City, Mis-

Glass 1-quart butter churn, 10½" tall, $300.00.

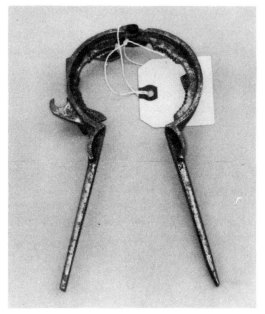

Cast-aluminum combination bottle and jar opener, marked "Uneek," 8" long, $35.00.

Rare cast-iron bean slicer with wooden knob, 7½" wide, $450.00.

Early egg sorter, circa 1860, tin with oak handle, 10" long, $225.00.

Cheese tester, handle marked "Imports & Milk Products," 17½" long, $18.00.

souri; United Royalties Corporation, New York City; and the Washburn Company, Worcester, Massachusetts.

Collectors of kitchen gadgets and utensils are fortunate in that these items can be found almost anywhere—from garage sales to antiques shows. With the exception of early primitives and those items considered rare, most of these small kitchen collectibles found today are very modestly priced.

Apple Parers

The advent of the apple parer was no doubt a blessing for cooks everywhere. Apples were a very important part of the diet during the eighteenth and nineteenth centuries, and whether apples were to be cooked, dried, or baked—the apple parer made preparation less tedious.

Early apple parers, such as the one patented by Mr. Moses Coates of Pennsylvania in 1803, were made of wood. To operate Mr. Coates's apple parer, the apple was placed on wooden prongs and then the fruit was rotated against a blade. Later apple parers were improved with the addition of gears.

By the mid-1800s apple parers also were being made of iron and metal and after 1850 they were mass produced of cast iron. Many different parers were patented and manufactured from the simple to the complicated, which were equipped

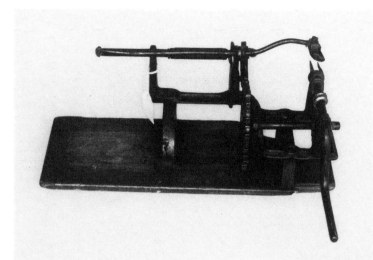

Iron apple parer on wooden board covered with original red paint, 18″ long, $145.00.

Apple parer, cast iron, marked "Pat. May 24, 1898, Turntable '98, Made by Goodell Co., USA, Antrim, N.H.," 10″ long, $68.00.

Turn-of-the-century rotary egg beater, unmarked, 9″ long, $20.00.

Beaters

Before the beater was developed it was left to a cook's imagination to devise a method of beating an egg. Miniature birch brooms and wooden paddles were employed but were difficult to clean. Forks also were used to beat eggs but were somewhat less than ideal for accomplishing the task.

The Industrial Revolution was responsible for numerous patented gadgets during the late 1800s and three types of egg beaters were among them: the rotary beater, the mechanical push beater, and the fixed wire whisk beater.

The Dover egg beater, a rotary beater made of iron and tin, was first patented in 1878. The Holts egg beater, which was patented in 1900, was also a rotary beater.

with handles, turntables, or gears. Some were designed to perform multiple tasks.

With the growing popularity of canned goods and "storeboughts" during the new century, the cast-iron apple parer slowly became obsolete. (Collectors should note that White Mountain Freezer Inc. of Massachusetts still manufacturers cast-iron apple parers.)

Dover egg beater, metal with wooden knob, 12″ long, $22.50.

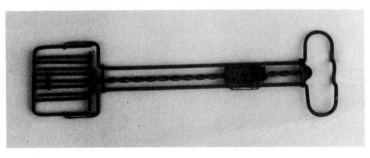

Unusual push-down whip marked "20th Century Egg & Cream Whip," all metal, 11″ tall, $29.00.

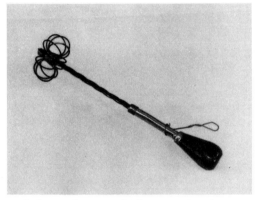

Push-down (plunger-style) beater with red wooden handle, 10½″ long, $75.00.

Keystone egg and cream beater, 2-cup size with tin beater and lid, 10″ tall (overall), $195.00.

The Holts beater had small blades surrounded by larger blades, and when the crank handle was turned, the blades rotated in opposite directions.

These assorted beaters were sold in hardware stores, emporiums, and through mail-order catalogs and were available in a "family" size of 10½″ or a "hotel" size of 12¼″.

The rotary "winged" beater was introduced by A&J Manufacturing of Binghamton, New York, in the early 1920s, and by 1926 an egg beater made entirely of tin had been patented and was quickly replacing the earlier models that had iron handles and cranks. These new tin models with their colorful wooden handles often were sold with a glass bowl and a tin cover that fit over the top. A&J Manufacturing produced numerous beater and bowl sets from the mid-1920s through the 1950s, using crystal or colored glass bowls or measuring cups.

Rotary beater with crock marked "Pat. 1916 Merry Whirl," beater has green wooden handle, 12" tall, $28.00.

Before the end of the 1920s, stainless steel egg beaters were being manufactured, and during the 1930s and 1940s they continued to have colorful wooden or enameled handles. For example, the 1932 Sears Roebuck catalog offered a double-action beater with enameled handle and knob for $0.22.

Can Openers

An increase in canned food products toward the end of the nineteenth century prompted inventors to create numerous gadgets for opening cans. The Peerless and the Delmonic can openers were patented in 1890, the Neverslip in 1892.

The Star Can Opener Company of California produced the thumbscrew opener in 1920, and by the late 1920s wall-mounted openers were being sold that

Wire beater marked "Enberry USA," 8" long, $1.00.

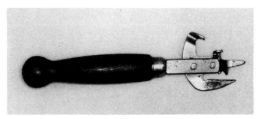

Can opener with wooden handle marked "Ekco, A&J USA," 6" long, $4.00.

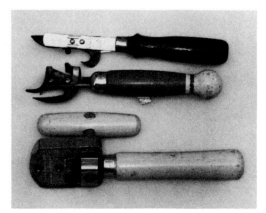

Can openers. Top: "Acme" with red wooden handle, 6" long, $5.00; Middle: opener marked "Acme Made in USA," 6" long, $5.00; Bottom: opener with yellow wooden handle and knob made by Edlund Co., Inc., Burlington, Vt., "#5 Jr.," 6" long, $6.00.

could open a can without leaving a jagged edge. It was, however, the multipurpose opener that remained popular, combining bottle and can openers with a cork screw in a single gadget.

The bottle openers and can openers of the 1930s and 1940s were made with colorful wooden handles and knobs.

Cast-iron cherry stoner marked "Enterprise Mfg. Co., Enterprise, Philadelphia," 12" long, $20.00.

Cherry Stoners

Cherry stoners, produced between 1880 and 1920, are truly a product of the Industrial Revolution and the all-out effort to bring efficiency and convenience to the kitchen.

Made of cast iron or tinned, cherry stoners were designed with legs for tabletop use or with a clamp so they could be attached to the table or cupboard.

In the early 1900s the Enterprise Manufacturing Company of Philadelphia, Pennsylvania, offered their japanned or tinned cherry stoners (design numbers 1, 2, 17, and 18) for $0.65 to $0.90. The No. 12 tinned stoner, according to *The Enterprising Housekeeper* cookbook, "is intended to stone cherries with the least possible cutting or disfiguring. Every good housewife will appreciate this for preserving purposes.... The most satisfactory results are obtained by dropping the cherries one at a time into the hopper immediately after [the] sweeper has passed the hole. With practice one can become expert." This model cost $1.25.

Cherry stoners were no longer a necessary gadget by the end of the 1920s due

Iron cherry stoner with clamp, unmarked, $30.00.

to the increase in the availability of packaged foods, preserves, and sweets.

Choppers, Grinders, and Graters

CHOPPERS AND GRINDERS

Choppers of some sort have been used for centuries to cut and mince fruits, meats, and vegetables. Early handmade choppers were turned out by the village

Choppers with wooden handles: left, 5¼" by 5½", $22.50; right, 5¼" by 4⅜", $18.00.

Nut meat chopper, "Androck," yellow lid, 6¼" tall, $7.00.

blacksmith or farmer and were rather simple and crude.

The Industrial Revolution introduced an assortment of factory-made choppers that had metal blades and wooden handles, but by the turn of the century choppers were being manufactured entirely of metal. The Eclipse Solid Steel Mincer and the Gem Solid Steel Mincer are two examples. Double-bladed choppers also were being produced after 1900.

During the 1920s and 1930s push-handle choppers with lids and glass jars or containers became available and had the advantages of being neat and containing odors. Rotary nut choppers also were being produced during this period. They consisted of a glass jar and turn-handle chopper, which allowed nuts to be cut and stored in the same container.

Iron and metal rotary meat grinders with turn handles became available during the early 1900s, and women enjoyed the convenience of this tool that could be clamped onto the Hoosier cabinet or the kitchen table. A bowl was placed underneath to catch whatever was being prepared.

During the early 1900s the Enterprise Manufacturing Company of Philadelphia, Pennsylvania, offered tinned meat and food choppers in several sizes, including a Small Family size, which could chop 1½ pounds per minute and cost $2.00; a Large Family size, which could chop 3 pounds per minute and cost $3.00; and the Butcher's size, which was capable of doing 4 pounds per minute and cost $6.00 new.

In one of their advertising cookbooks Enterprise stated that "Anything that is chopped into pieces for food is legitimate material to pass through a Food Chopper, and when once a Cook or Housekeeper realizes the efficiency and utility of an Enterprise Food Chopper, she will never be without one, nor use a substitute. . . . These were designed with a view of making a Chopper so simple as not to require directions how to use, and therefore especially adapted for family use."

GRATERS

Graters of simple punched tin preceded the factory-made examples produced from the late 1800s on into the new century. These hand-held tools were used by rubbing the foodstuff against the rough surface, which caused shredding. Initially hand graters were made with wooden handles and in assorted sizes from very small to quite large.

Small nutmeg graters were popular during the late 1800s for adding flavor to drinks. The Edgar Nutmeg Grater, which was patented in 1891, held the nutmeg in place with a spring while the spice was moved back and forth against the grater.

Although the factory-made metal kitchen grater was popular during the early 1900s (and continues to be sold today), there was also a clamp-on style grater being sold during the 1920s and 1930s. A 1930 advertisement for the Climax grater and slicer by Hamilton Metal Products Company of Ohio told readers, "quickly cuts fruits and vegetables into wafer-thin slices that melt in your mouth. Grater, attached in a jiffy, grates cheese,

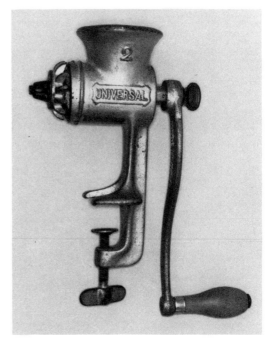

Universal meat grinder with wooden knob on handle, 8½" long, $30.00.

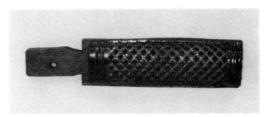

Small, early grater, 6¼" long, $30.00.

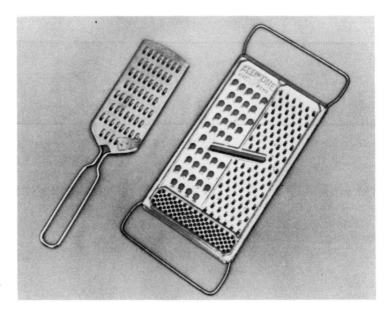

Graters. Left: handle marked "Nutbrown, Stainless Steel, Made in England," 9¼" long, $1.00; Right: large grater marked "All in One, Pat. Pending," 10½" long, $1.00.

84

Edgar nutmeg grater, $85.00.

crackers, carrots, etc. without crushing. No cut fingers. Sanitary, durable. Thousands in use. Glass block, easily cleaned, prevents flavor taint—no splinters. Choice of red, blue, green, white." The Climax with glass block sold for $2.00.

Coffee Grinders

Coffee was a luxury item during the 1700s; therefore, coffee grinders did not become a household utensil until the nineteenth century. By that time coffee was readily

Rare barrel-type nutmeg grater marked "Iron— Patented June 1870," $215.00.

Early 1880s mortise-and-tenon coffee mill with brass hopper, 7″ wide by 4″ high, $200.00.

Climax grater, tin and iron with wooden lid, marked "Climax, Hamilton, Ohio, Pat. Pend.," 8″ tall, $12.00.

85

Unusual (possibly English) coffee grinder with smokestack funnel and locking drawer, 5" wide by 8" tall, $225.00.

Universal coffee mill, No. 109 by Landers, Frary, and Clark, 5" wide by 6½" high, $60.00.

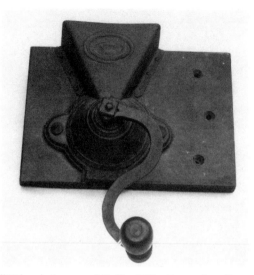

"Wilson's Improved Coffee Mill—Patent," wall-mount unit, 8" long, $38.00.

available and less expensive because of improved trade with coffee-exporting countries.

Coffee grinders of the late 1800s through the early twentieth century were factory-made of iron, wood, and japanned tin. Some were known as X-ray coffee grinders because they had glass fronts and could be attached to a wall.

The wooden, box-style grinder was very popular for home use and was manufactured by a number of different companies.

The Sun No. 42 Improved Coffee Mill by the Sun Manufacturing Company, Columbus, Ohio, is an example of a plain wooden coffee grinder with a wooden bottom drawer and cast-iron swinging cover with a handle.

The Parker Company of Meriden, Connecticut, sold a decorative coffee grinder called Parker's National Coffee Mill No. 430. This kitchen tool was wooden with coppered iron castings.

A third company, Landers, Frary and Clark, sold a functional Universal Coffee Mill that had a steel case with a black enamel finish. Their Crown No. 1 model was more elaborate, having a black enamel finish and a brass sliding cover.

The 1908 Sears Roebuck catalog offered the Home Box Coffee Mill for $0.52 and the glass front X-ray Wall Coffee Mill was $0.47.

The Enterprise Manufacturing Company offered several Rapid Grinding and Pulverizing Mills, including a side mill

Arcade glass coffee grinder, 14½″ long, $65.00.

that was screwed to the kitchen wall (cost $1.25), a model that could be clamped to a table or cupboard (cost $1.50), and several different tabletop mills that cost between $2.25 and $5.00. "All [are] highly ornamented and handsome in appearance."

According to *The Enterprising Housekeeper*, the advertising cookbook distributed by the Enterprise Manufacturing Company, "A coffee mill is a household necessity if one wishes good coffee. . . . In selecting a coffee mill it is better to take one that stands on a shelf or table, than those screwed upon the wall. The former are more apt to be cleaned often, require less time to operate, and save all the coffee and its strength."

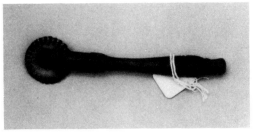

Small bone crimper with wooden handle, 5″ long, $30.00.

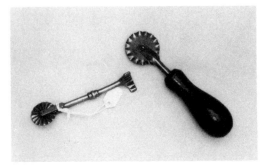

Pie crimpers. Left: small brass crimper, 4″ long, $18.00; Right: larger brass crimper with black wooden handle, 5″ long, $8.00.

Crimpers and Cookie Cutters

CRIMPERS

Pastry crimpers have been used by bakers for centuries to cut pastry, seal pie crusts, and for fluting pie edges.

The early crimpers used to prepare popular meat pies and fruit pies were made of wood, wrought iron, brass, whale bone, ivory, and porcelain. By the turn of the century, crimpers were factory made of tin. During the 1920s through the 1940s,

they were made of aluminum with colored wooden handles.

COOKIE CUTTERS

Nineteenth-century tinsmiths created whimsical cookie cutters from leftover scraps of tin. Made in the shapes of hearts, stars, people, and animals, cookie cutters were especially popular for creating special treats for holidays.

Old tin cookie cutters: round shape on the right, 4", $7.00; bird on the left, 4", $8.00.

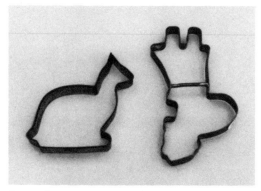

Tin cookie cutters: cat on the left, 3" tall by 2½" wide, $8.00; Santa on the right, 4" tall by 2¾" wide, $15.00.

Cookie cutters with red and green wooden knobs, 2½", each $2.00.

After 1900, cookie cutters were factory made and were often sold in sets. For example, the 1932 Sears Roebuck catalog offered a dozen animal-shaped cutters for $0.45. From the 1920s through the 1940s cookie cutters were made with colorful wooden or metal knobs.

Ice cream freezer, unmarked, wood with original blue paint, 15" high by 12" wide, $25.00.

A small, 1-quart Alaska ice cream freezer, marked "Made in the USA," 9" tall, $34.00.

Ice Cream Gadgets and Utensils

ICE CREAM FREEZERS

Ice cream was a favorite treat during the Victorian era and was commercially prepared and sold by 1850. A small ice cream freezer for home use was invented in 1864 by Nancy Johnson. This wooden tub with an inner box for freezing the cream was operated with a churn crank.

An 1889 advertisement for the Peerless ice cream freezer made by the Gooch Freezer Co., Cincinnati, Ohio.

By 1900 a variety of wooden and metal turn-handle ice cream freezers were being factory made by several different companies including the White Mountain Freezer Company, Nashua, New Hampshire; the Mammoth Foundry, Buffalo, New York; North Brothers Manufacturing Company, Philadelphia, Pennsylvania (produced Shepard's Lightning Freezer); Acme Can Company of Philadelphia, Pennsylvania (Acme Five-Minute Freezer); the Dana Manufacturing Company, Cincinnati, Ohio (Dana Peerless Freezer); and the Gooch Freezer Company, Cincinnati, Ohio.

Home ice cream freezers continued to be used through the 1920s, which by then were made entirely of metal.

ICE CREAM DISHERS

In order to serve the popular nineteenth-century ice cream, "dishers," or scoops, were manufactured to remove the treat from its container.

William Clewell of Reading, Pennsylvania, is credited with inventing the first mechanical ice cream disher in 1876. This cone-shaped disher with a turn-release mechanism was made of tin and became known as Clad's Disher, named after the tinsmith that manufactured Clewell's invention.

Other dishers soon were patented by eager inventors, including the 1890 Rapid Disher that could be operated with one hand, thanks to a squeeze-handle release mechanism. Dishers were made in an assortment of round and oval shapes. Nickel-plated brass became more popular than

Early tin ice cream disher with turn knob, 8″ long, $18.00.

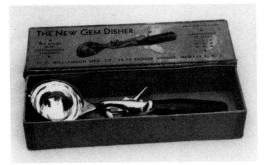

Ice cream disher or scoop, "The New Gem Disher," with original box, wooden handle, 9½″ long, $85.00.

the less-sanitary tin and steel for making these gadgets.

After 1900 many companies were producing dishers or scoops, including the Kingery Company (Rapid Disher), Cincinnati, Ohio; V. Clad and Sons, Philadelphia, Pennsylvania; Gem Spoon Company, Troy, New York; and the Dover Manufacturing Company, Dover, New Hampshire.

Collectors find common scoops in-

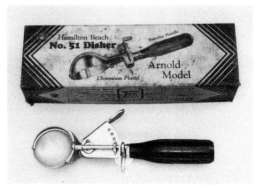

Hamilton Beach No. 51 disher with original box, chromium plated and Bakelite handle, 8½″ long, $32.00.

Pewter valentine ice cream mold, 4″ across, $46.00.

Two-piece pewter ice cream mold, the pair, $155.00.

Pewter flag ice cream mold, marked "E & Co," 5¼″ long, $75.00; American Eagle mold (open), marked "S & Co," 5¼″ long, $95.00.

Pewter ice cream mold, grapes (open), 5″ long, $38.00.

expensive while rare ones or those with unusual features can cost more than $100.00.

ICE CREAM MOLDS

Pewter ice cream molds were used in the commercial production of ice cream from the 1850s through the 1920s. These molds were made in a variety of shapes and sizes, including holiday motifs, fruits, flowers, vegetables, and other novelties such as the patriotic eagle, which is considered quite rare today.

Three northeastern companies became the largest manufacturers of molds in America: Schall and Company of New York City, Eppelsheimer and Company of New York City, and Fr. Krauss of Pennsylvania. Ice cream molds also were made by smaller companies such as J. Ernst of New York City, and they were imported from European manufacturers as well.

With increasing labor and production costs, companies that commercially prepared shapely ice cream treats found it was no longer a profitable venture. As a result, the use of ice cream molds was discontinued. While many of these molds were probably scrapped, just as many were boxed and stored away only to be discovered years later. Today we find ice cream molds at antiques shops and flea markets, often mixed in with other kitchen collectibles. With the exception of rare examples, most can be purchased for well under $100.

Juicers

Juice extractors have been used for centuries, and with the introduction of citrus groves in America during the 1700s, the wooden reamer-style juicer became popular.

During the 1800s a wooden, two-part hinged mechanical reamer was handmade and then later factory produced in metal.

The Industrial Revolution ushered in numerous juicers including Easley's 1888 glass juicer, which had a cone-shaped

Blue enamelware lemon juicer, 6″ long, $48.00.

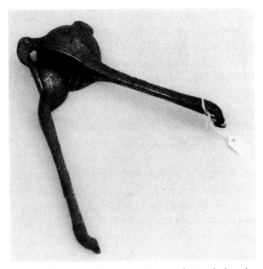

Unusual cast-iron lemon juicer with rippled end that was rolled over the lemon to loosen the rind, marked ''Pat. Pending,'' 9″ long, $185.00.

Aluminum lemon juicer, unmarked, 9″ long, $22.00.

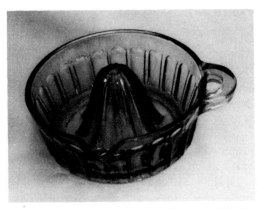

Green depression glass reamer, 7½″ across, $20.00.

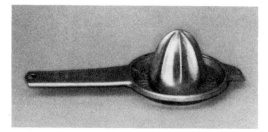

Aluminum juicer, marked "Aluminum Pat. 161609 Mpls, Minn," 8″ long, $2.00.

projection on a saucer. This style remained popular during this past century and continues to be used today.

After 1900 oranges and grapefruit became more available, and juicers became an important kitchen tool. They were made of cast iron, tin, glass, aluminum, and enamelware.

While the reamer-style juicer remained popular, numerous mechanical juicers were manufactured that involved pressing down on or turning a handle to extract the juice, which would be deposited in a cup or attached container.

Glassware juicers from the 1920s through the 1950s are extremely popular and were made in a variety of colors. Cobalt blue, amber, and pink are scarce, highly collectible, and can cost hundreds of dollars. White, green, and crystal reamers still can be found at flea markets, house sales, and antiques shows and shops and are more modestly priced.

Mortars and Pestles

Mortars and pestles of various sizes have been used by cooks for centuries to crush herbs, spices, salt, sugar, and coffee beans. A strong, hard material that resists scratching and breaking is used to make this utensil, including wood, marble, stoneware, and iron. Marble and stoneware mortars and pestles are associated with the apothecary, which used them to make medicines and prescriptions during the nineteenth century.

Wooden mortar and pestle, 6″ tall by 5″ wide, $70.00.

Mortars and pestles usually turn up at antiques shows and interested collectors should check with dealers who display primitives and kitchenware from the nineteenth century.

Nutcrackers

Prior to the invention of the nutcracker, our resourceful forefathers used hammers to crack almonds, walnuts, butternuts, chestnuts, and pecans.

During the 1800s cast-iron nut crackers in animal shapes became the rage. The nut was placed in the animal's open mouth and by pressing the animal's tail the nut was crushed.

Brass nutcrackers were quite popular with Victorians, who included them in dining room place settings. Their bright shine complimented the elegant tableware while the black cast-iron examples stayed in the kitchen.

In 1889 a nickel-plated steel nutcracker with a squeeze handle was pat-

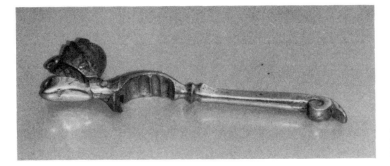

Jolly Jester nutcracker, nut is placed in jester's mouth, 6" long, $20.00.

Late 1940s nutcracker and matching pick, $1.00.

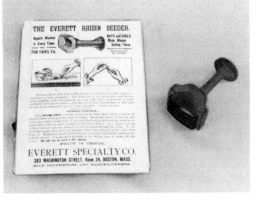

Late 1800s small wooden Everett raisin seeder with original box, 3¼" long, $80.00.

ented, and 1916 saw the introduction of a lever-operated gadget marked the "Home Nut Cracker—Made in St. Louis, U.S.A." The squeeze-handle nutcracker has remained popular through the years and is still being used today.

Raisin Seeders

Many puddings and pies called for raisins as a key ingredient and during the 1800s numerous raisin seeders were patented during the height of the gadget craze.

Some models were quite large, made of cast iron, and could be clamped to the tabletop, but other small, hand-held seeders also were available. With all models, the raisins were pressed against wires to remove the seeds.

The raisin seeder disappeared with the advent of packaged foods, preserves, and baked goods, but collectors can find these more unusual kitchen gadgets at antiques shops and shows, especially from dealers who specialize in kitchenware and primitives.

Rolling Pins

Wooden rolling pins of some form have been used for centuries. These utensils usually were homemade until they began to be factory produced in the mid-nineteenth century. Wooden rolling pins were made of maple, apple, cherry, walnut, and pine.

A special type of wooden rolling pin was used to create a German Christmas cookie called a *Springerle*. These rolling pins have flowers, fruits, and various other designs hand carved in squares on the utensil.

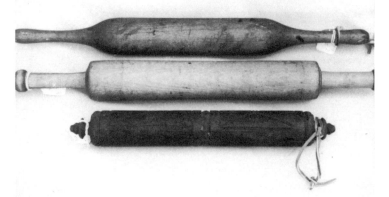

Wooden rolling pins. Top: maple rolling pin, 17″ long, $45.00; Middle: maple rolling pin, 17″ long, $28.00; Bottom: small carved walnut rolling pin, 12″ long, $65.00.

Stoneware rolling pin with cobalt blue bands, 14½″ long, $325.00.

Rare tin rolling pin with wooden handles, 17″ long, $325.00.

Glass rolling pin with label intact, "Columbus Baking Powder," tin cap on one end, 12″ long, $240.00.

Stoneware and yellowware rolling pins also were made during the nineteenth century, and today these scarce examples cost hundreds of dollars. Porcelain and glass rolling pins were manufactured that could be filled with cold water to chill the dough. They were easy to clean and often were very decorative. They also were used as advertising giveaways. For example, a woman might buy a rolling pin filled with baking powder that, once emptied of its contents, made a handy kitchen utensil.

Depression glass rolling pins were

Wooden rolling pin, 20″ long, $18.00.

U.S. Family Scale with brass face, marked "Pat. 1898," 10″ tall, $68.00.

American Family Scale marked "Peck & Mack Co. New York, Oct. 29, 1912," japanned tin with gold-and-black trim around face, 9¼″ tall, $10.00.

made during the 1930s and 1940s in an assortment of colors. Today collectors will find these glass collectibles cost hundreds of dollars.

Over the years the wooden rolling pin has remained popular and most widely used. In 1932 the Sears Roebuck catalog offered polished hardwood rolling pins for $0.32 each.

House sales, flea markets, auctions, and antiques shows are excellent opportunities for locating old rolling pins. They are often boxed with other kitchenware, especially at auctions. Common wooden examples from the late nineteenth and early twentieth centuries can be had for

a modest price whereas scarce examples will cost hundreds of dollars.

Scales

With the 1896 publication of the *Boston Cooking School Cook Book* by Fannie Farmer, cooks became interested in obtaining small scales to be more precise in measuring ingredients. As a result, the Acme Household Scale and the American Family Scale became available for household use in the early 1900s. These smaller

American Family Scale, cream colored, 8" tall, $15.00.

Egg scale with orange, green, yellow, and red ranges, marked "Jiffy Way, U.S. Pat. No. 2,205,917," $40.00.

Acme egg grading scale, "Acme, St. Paul, Minn.," $25.00.

scale graded eggs according to their weight and was made of metal with plain or painted markings on the side.

Old household scales can be found at flea markets, yard sales, and antiques shops and shows. Look for scales in good condition, with very little rust, and with labels or advertisements intact.

Sifters

Several tin sifters were patented during the second half of the nineteenth century, replacing the crude wooden and pierced tin sifters and strainers that had been used until that time. The patented sifters included Earnshaw's patent of 1866, the Bucknam Improved Combination sifter, and the 1879 Hunter sifter.

The July 1889 *Harper's New Monthly* magazine contained an advertisement for the Hunter sifter by the Fred J. Meyers Manufacturing Company of Covington, Kentucky, which told readers "pulverized sugar is almost always lumpy. Before using it for sweetening fresh berries, sliced peaches, oranges, pine-apples and other fruits, it should be rubbed through a Hunter sifter. Sugar of this sort always should be sifted. The Hunter sifter is for sale at stove, hardware, and house-furnishing stores."

From the turn of the century through the 1920s the rotary, or turn-handle, sifter was in use. The squeeze-handle

tools were advertised as being light, compact, and convenient.

The 1924 Montgomery Ward catalog offered an assortment of scales for the home, including the Little Detective Scale, made of steel with a white enameled dial, which sold for $1.98. The Blue Beauty scale, made of "the best rolled steel and finished in blue enamel," was priced at $2.89.

Another popular type of scale used in the early 1900s was the egg scale. The egg

Early tin scoop with turn-handle sifter, $125.00.

Large rotary sifter, Belmont, black wooden knob on handle, 7″ tall by 5″ wide, $29.00.

Androck "Hand-i-sift" flour sifter with red wooden squeeze handle, 5½″ tall by 5″ wide, $30.00.

Small squeeze-handle sifter, marked "Savory Junior," tin with bands of green trim, 5″ tall by 4″ wide, $8.00.

sifter was then introduced and immediately became popular because it allowed the cook a free hand for mixing, stirring, and so forth.

In 1929 Meets-a-Need Manufacturing Company of Seattle, Washington, advertised their Sift-Chine, which was "not an ordinary flour sifter, but a sifting machine . . . one hand operates—quickly—easily." The Sift-Chine was available with green, red, yellow, or blue handles and cost $1.00.

All-metal sifters were available during the 1930s and 1940s and collectors find these make desirable additions to a kitchenware collection along with examples of the earlier styles.

Trivets

Trivets were a necessary utensil with multiple uses. Primitive trivets were used at the hearth to support the kettle and pots that were used over the fire. Smaller,

Iron trivets. Left: "Best on Earth," 7¼" long, $27.00; Right: "'I Want U' Comfort Iron Strause Gas Iron Co., Philadelphia, Pa., U.S.A.," 7" long, $29.00.

Triangular iron trivet on feet (for fireplace cooking), 7" long, $59.00.

Ceramic and wire trivet with ornate wirework design, marked "Stoke on Trent, Mintons China Works," 6" by 6", $65.00.

cast-iron trivets were factory made during the 1800s to support hot sadirons. They often were made in a spade shape to match the irons they supported. Trivets also were used as hot plates during the late 1800s through the early 1900s. They were made of pottery, wire, brass, nickel plate, or tile and supported hot dishes on the table.

Collectors find it is the cast-iron sadiron trivet of the nineteenth century that turns up most often at flea markets and antiques shops, because they were mass produced and were being used well into the 1930s before electric irons gained in popularity.

Washday Tools

WASHBOARDS

Prior to the mid-nineteenth century, wooden corrugated washboards were made by hand and often were carved from a single piece of wood. Very primitive in appearance, they served the purpose and

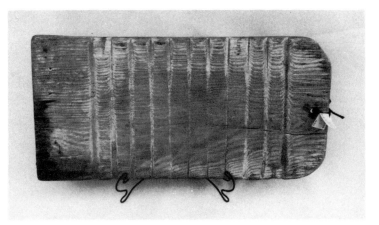

Early hand-carved washboard,
19½″ long by 10″ wide, $125.00.

Blue speckled graniteware washboard, 24″ tall by
12½″ wide, $55.00.

Glass washboard marked "Two in One Glass,
Mfg. by Carolina Washboard Co., Raleigh, N.C.,
No. 80," 24″ long by 12″ wide, $15.00.

were used every Monday when the wooden washtub or copper boiler was filled with hot water for what was called washday.

Early factory-made spool-shaped wooden washboards became popular by the 1850s and several potteries also produced yellowware and Rockingham washboards along with their other utilitarian goods.

Factory-made washboards that were produced from the late 1800s on were made of zinc, brass, glass, and graniteware. After the turn of the century they also were made with aluminum-coated steel and sheet metal scrubbing surfaces.

Many companies produced washboards of various sizes (small washboards made during the early 1900s were

Copper boiler with lid,
23″ long by 13″ high, $95.00.

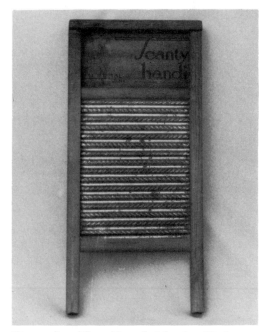

"Scanty handi" washboard, Columbus Washboard Co., Columbus, Ohio, marked "Ideal for silks, hosiery & lingerie," 18″ long by 8½″ wide, $12.00.

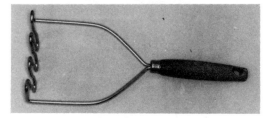

Wire masher with wooden handle, 10½″ long, $2.00.

WRINGERS

Wooden wringers were designed to clamp onto the washtub to wring out wet clothing before hanging it up to dry. They operated by a crank-handle that turned wooden or, later, rubber rollers.

The American Wringer Company of New York produced several wooden wringers in the early 1900s, including the Marvel, Daisy, Paragon, and Relief. They could be clamped onto the sink or washtub and had standard wooden rollers.

More costly, high-grade wringers also were made, including a model with rubber rollers called the Royal, which had a hardwood frame and was warranted for five years.

Wire Mashers

Mashers, like several other kitchen tools, have been used for centuries. Early mash-

for undergarments) and of assorted materials. Companies included the National Washboard Company, Chicago, Illinois; Columbus Washboard Company, Columbus, Ohio; Wayne Manufacturing Company, St. Louis, Missouri; and Richmond Cedar Works, Richmond, Virginia.

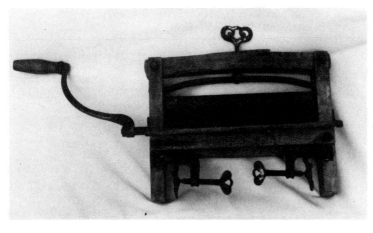

Wringer with rubber rollers, marked "Lorell No. 32," $9.00.

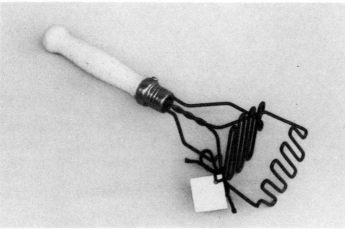

Unusual two-tier wire masher with white wooden handle, marked "Pat. 4/18/12," 11″ long, $59.00.

Wooden beetle, 11″ long, $8.00.

ers were made of wood (usually maple) and in many different sizes depending on the task for which they were created. By the mid-1800s wire mashers with wooden handles were replacing the all-wood masher. These remained popular through the turn of the century.

During the 1920s and 1930s an assortment of mashers was manufactured with round or square stainless steel heads or zigzag wires. These mashers displayed the various colored wooden handles that remained popular throughout the 1940s.

Wirework

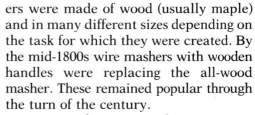

Iron and steel wirework, or wire goods, were very popular during the second half of the nineteenth century. Manufacturers

Wire pie rack, $65.00; pie fork with wooden handle, $60.00.

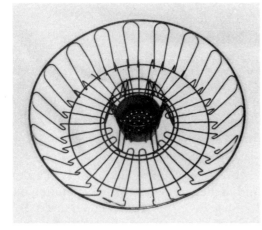

Wire dish strainer, $55.00.

Wire rack for cooking eggs, $48.00.

gave Victorian women a variety of kitchenware items to use including baskets, dish drainers, rug beaters, tea balls, iron trivets, corn poppers, wire- and wooden-handled strainers, toasters, and wire dish covers.

Most wirework sold through catalogs, and although some of these items became obsolete, others continue to be manufactured today. Collectors find old wirework items readily available and modestly priced, with the exception of rare or unusual pieces, such as a set of round or oval dish covers, which were sold in assorted sizes, very ornate baskets, and compotes.

CHAPTER 6 Kitchen Furniture

Turn-of-the-century bakers' cabinets, multipurpose Hoosier kitchen cabinets, and colorful, decorative breakfast sets have captured the attention of antiques enthusiasts and collectors. This twentieth-century kitchen furniture is being viewed with newfound respect as it quickly approaches one hundred years in age. But it is both significant and highly collectible for another, more important, reason.

When convenience became the driving force behind invention during the late 1800s, it was the hoosier-style kitchen cabinet that revolutionized the kitchen. A direct descendant of the bakers' cabinet, the hoosier cabinet combined multiple functions with a centralized work area to bring organization to the kitchen. A woman could now do her work efficiently and more quickly.

Today these assorted cabinets and vintage 1920 to 1940s breakfast sets are finding their way back into our kitchens

and many are being used as originally intended.

The Bakers' Cabinet

The late 1800s saw factory-made bakers' tables being sold commercially through furniture stores and mail-order catalogs. The bakers' table was a work center for the cook, a place where she could roll dough, slice bread, and perform any number of kitchen chores. Flour and sugar could be stored in the bin drawers underneath the table for easy access.

By the late 1890s a top piece for storing spices, utensils, and dishes had been added to the table, and these work centers were called bakers' cabinets.

There were cabinets of various styles and sizes, made from assorted woods. For example, the 1908 Sears Roebuck catalog offered several cabinets, including their basic Big Bargain cabinet, which was 50″ tall, made of white maple, and cost $5.45 new. The more elaborate models ranged in price from $7.85 to $12.95.

Continued improvement and addi-

A black-and-white advertisement for Sellers kitchen cabinets published in the October 1925 *Ladies' Home Journal.*

A turn-of-the-century bakers' cabinet, pine and maple wood, 48″ wide by 60″ tall, $700.00.

tions to the bakers' cabinet led to the development of the larger, more modern hoosier-style kitchen cabinet, which became the epitome of efficiency during the early 1900s through the 1920s.

Hoosier Kitchen Cabinets

The advent of industrialization and the great strides being made to bring modern convenience to the kitchen led to a new concept in efficiency—the single-unit kitchen cabinet.

Storage needs for cooking utensils, dishes, pots and pans, and food staples were organized into this single unit. It was a step-saving, multipurpose work center. Manufactured from 1899 through the 1930s, the kitchen cabinet was made in assorted sizes and models by numer-

ous companies and advertised as a helpmate, full of handy facilities, offering beauty and convenience in the kitchen, introducing the new era of housewifery, and so on.

The 1919 *Ladies' Home Journal* included an advertisement by the Hoosier Manufacturing Company that stated, "Retain your youthful energy and girlish appearance," the wedding-day advice of thousands of mothers. "As they look back over the years, they realize that woman's charms soon fade and her health often gives way when drudgery methods rule her days."

The Mutschler Brothers Company,

Oak cabinet by the Hoosier Mfg. Co., with frosted glass cupboard doors, pull-down flour bin in the top left cupboard, white porcelain-enamel work area with blue trim, 40" wide by 70" tall, $750.00.

Kitchen cabinet, manufacturer unknown, three frosted glass top cupboard doors, middle doors open to flour bin and additional storage, wooden work surface is a replacement piece, light oak finish, 40" wide by 70" tall, $600.00.

A 1925 advertisement for the Hoosier Highboy.

A 1928 color advertisement for Sellers "Kitchenaire," which was available in several popular colors.

Nappanee, Indiana; Showers Brothers Company, Bloomington, Indiana; the McDougall Company, Frankfort, Indiana; Ingram Richardson, Frankfort, Indiana; Sellers and Sons Company, Elwood, Indiana; Boone Cabinets, Lebanon, Indiana; and the Hoosier Manufacturing Company, New Castle, Indiana, were just a few of the many companies that manufactured these time-saving units. Due to the fact that so many of them were located in Indiana, the cabinets became generally known as hoosier cabinets.

A 1925 advertisement for Sellers and Sons kitchen cabinets proclaimed "of all scientific devices tending to liberate women from day-long drudgery, it is the modern kitchen cabinet. By this remarkable stride in domestic engineering, the preparation of good foods is changed from a heavy task to a fine accomplishment."

As a concentrated work center, basic kitchen cabinets were designed to provide for the housewife's every need in the kitchen. Standard features included storage space for dishes and cooking utensils,

a metal bin with sifter for up to 50 pounds of flour, a metal bread drawer with a ventilating lid, breadboard, recipe box, silverware drawer, spice rack and jars, and a sliding aluminum or porcelain enamel extension top. Basic cabinets were available in an oak or enamel paint (white, gray, and green) finish.

Deluxe model kitchen cabinets often were larger, having additional cupboard space and extra features such as canister sets and a swing-out ironing board.

From the early 1900s through the 1920s a deluxe cabinet was decorated with frosted glass cupboard doors or doors with slag glass inserts.

The art deco Hoosier of the late 1920s through the 1930s often had geometric stenciled designs on the cupboard doors. For example, the 1930 Hoosier Manufacturing Company catalog offered a cabinet in gray enamel with rose and black decorations; the old ivory cabinet had orange and blue decorations; and the spring green

A Sellers kitchen cabinet with slag glass inserts in top cupboard doors, tambour door hides storage area, oak finish, circa 1920s, 40" wide by 70" tall, $600.00.

painted cabinet was decorated with red and black.

This particular company, the Hoosier Manufacturing Company, founded in 1899 by J. S. McQuinn, was the most noted of the cabinetmaking companies. They made and sold more cabinets than any other company in America, and they advertised extensively to promote "a Hoosier for every type of kitchen."

To meet the needs of every type of kitchen, the Hoosier Company manufactured cabinets in several sizes. A 1908 catalog advertised a cabinet that was "larger than any of the other patterns and

does away with the need of a pantry." This particular unit was 67" high by 52" wide—a foot wider than the standard size.

A 1925 advertisement offered the Hoosier Highboy, an unusually tall unit, and a 1930 catalog offered the Hoosier Junior, a 36"-wide model. They also advertised a cabinet that was small enough to fit under a window.

Because a kitchen cabinet was actually a piece of furniture, and indeed an investment for any homemaker, most companies offered to arrange terms for customers. A 1923 Hoosier Company advertisement stated "the best news of all is the fact that you do not need to go on doing your work in the hard, old-fashioned way while you save up money to buy the Hoosier. Your dealer will put the Hoosier in your home on dignified, easy terms."

The Hoosier Manufacturing Company was quite successful during their forty-three years of production. The company closed in 1942.

Another well-known kitchen cabinet was manufactured by Sellers and Sons. The G.I. Sellers kitchen cabinets were made by the Elwood Furniture Manufacturing Company of Elwood, Indiana, from 1902 through the 1930s.

The greatest number of Sellers cabinets was sold during the 1920s while production was at its peak. The company offered different model cabinets, including the June Bride and Sellers Kitcheneed Special, and also produced a line of cabinets sold through the Montgomery Ward catalog.

The craftsmen employed by Elwood Furniture are credited with bringing innovations to cabinetmaking. Examples include the pull-down flour bin and the ant-proof castor, which was a molded metal cup around the wheel castor that was filled with water to prevent ants from getting into food stored in the cupboards.

Sales of Sellers kitchen cabinets fell off in the 1930s and the company ceased production of their furniture lines in 1949. The plant closed two years later.

A third extremely successful manufacturer of kitchen cabinets was the Campbell-Smith-Ritchie Company of Lebanon, Indiana. What began as a planing mill and lumberyard in the late 1800s grew to include the manufacture of furniture such as kitchen cabinets, wardrobes, and cupboards by 1907.

The lumberyard aspect of the business was discontinued in 1910 because of the overwhelming popularity of the kitchen cabinets that the company was producing.

The Boone kitchen cabinet was avail-

A 1927 advertisement for the Mary Boone model cabinet by the Campbell-Smith-Ritchie Co. of Lebanon, Ind.

able in three models. The Mary Boone, which was the top of the line, had special features like a built-in desk, an alarm clock, a disappearing ironing board, and an optional Arcade Crystal Coffee Mill; it sold for $50.00 to $75.00. The second model, the Helen Boone, offered many of the same features as the Mary Boone but was smaller in size and was finished in golden oak instead of white paint. The Helen Boone sold for $40.00 to $50.00. The Dorothy Boone, a much smaller model, was intended to be used underneath a kitchen window and cost $25.00 to $30.00.

The Boone cabinets were sold mainly throughout the Midwest. After the sale of kitchen cabinets dropped, the company went on to make the built-in cabinets that became popular in kitchens during the late 1930s, along with kitchen tables and chairs. The company was sold in 1940 and closed two years later.

Continued efforts to bring organiza-

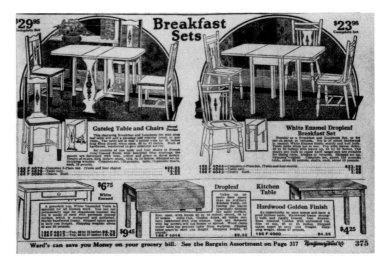

A variety of breakfast sets and tables available in the summer 1924 Montgomery Ward catalog.

tion and efficiency to the kitchen resulted in streamlined designs during the 1930s. Work areas were recommended by the stove, sink, and refrigerator. The result was built-in kitchen cabinets—wall and floor units with a continuous countertop. By the late 1930s the freestanding hoosier kitchen cabinet was no longer being assembled.

Many old hoosier cabinets still reside in basements, attics, and garages. Watch for them to turn up at auctions and estate sales. Antiques shows and antiques dealers who carry oak furniture or specialize in kitchenware are excellent sources for locating a hoosier in nice original condition or one that has been restored. Prices depend on the cabinet's condition, equipment, size, and decorative features such as glass cupboard doors. The type of wood used to make the cabinet also will affect the cabinet's price.

Kitchenette or "Breakfast Nook" Sets

The breakfast nook was a small area or alcove off the kitchen in homes built dur-

ing the 1920s and 1930s. It was the ideal spot for family meals, and furniture manufacturers wasted no time in filling the need for a table and chair set that would blend with the informal atmosphere of the kitchen.

In 1924 the Hoosier Manufacturing Company of Indiana advertised their breakfast set as "daintily finished in white enamel and decorated in bright colors, the table has a fine porcelain top and the chairs have cane seats."

Many of the same companies that manufactured hoosier kitchen cabinets also made kitchen table and chair sets. These drop-leaf, or extension, tables were offered with an enamel paint finish or a wooden finish with painted-on accent trim. Color became an important factor in kitchen design during the 1920s and as a result, these small, painted table and chair sets became very popular.

Along with the companies that manufactured kitchen cabinets, other manufacturers of breakfast sets included the Phoenix Chair Company, Sheboygan, Wisconsin; St. John's Table Company, Cadillac, Michigan; and the Shreve Chair Company, Incorporated, Union City, Pennsylvania. There were numerous others.

Buffets, Welsh cupboards, and serv-

Porcelain-enamel top table, white with green trim and tabletop design, four art deco chairs purchased with table, complete set $95.00.

Blue enamel-top table, and four blue chairs, the complete set is $275.00.

ers were made to match the breakfast nook set and also were intended for use in the kitchen.

The 1924 Montgomery Ward *Spring and Summer Catalog* offered a comlete five-piece (table and four chairs) gateleg table set with floral design for $29.95. It was advertised as "charming Breakfast and Luncheon Set with dropleaf table . . . will add a pleasing and colorful touch to any room." The set was avail-

able in French gray enamel finish with blue shading and a rose, yellow, and green floral design on the chair backs and table legs.

By the 1930s the influence of stream-lining kitchens resulted in more modern-istic table and chair sets with Monel Metal tops and chrome-plated legs. These sets were available with white, ivory, green, or black trim.

During the late 1940s colorful di-

Marie Louise breakfast set, complete with table, chairs, and optional server, from the 1924 Montgomery Ward catalog, designed in Dutch gray enamel with Holland blue trim, $59.95 new. "Napanee Dutch Kitchenet, Nappanee, Indiana."

nette sets were made from chrome with laminated plastic on the tabletops and plastic upholstery on the seats. Chromcraft Dinette Furniture by the American Fixture and Manufacturing Company of St. Louis, Missouri, and Daystrom Furniture of Olean, New York, and Pasadena, California, were leading manufacturers of chrome furniture.

These table and chair sets are increasingly being seen at antiques shows and interested collectors also can check with dealers who specialize in art deco or modernistic furniture.

CHAPTER 7 Pottery

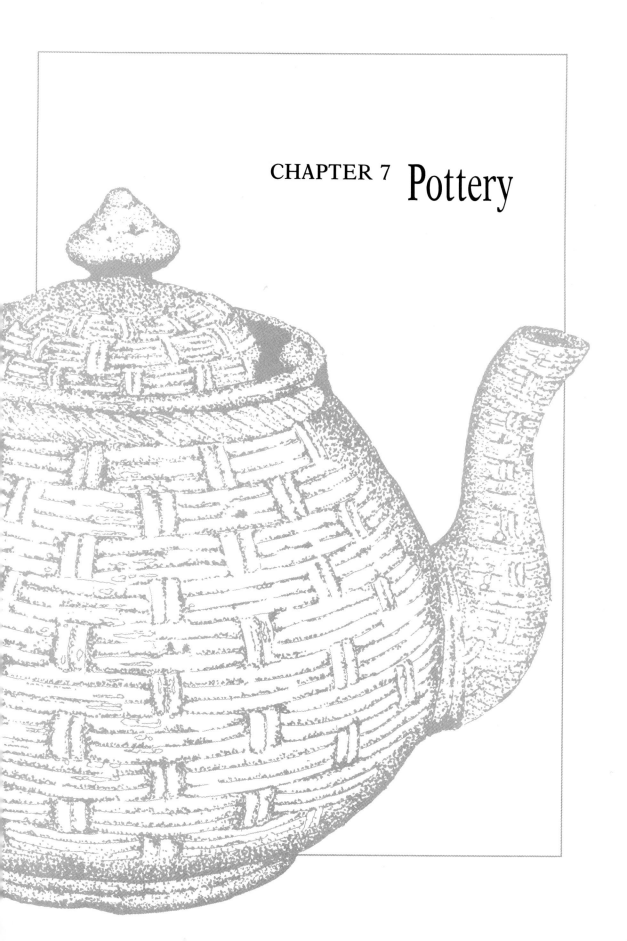

Collectors have discovered during the last twenty years that there is something quite special about the utilitarian, often primitive early pottery created in America. Redware and stoneware are enthusiastically collected and appreciated for the simple folk art designs that were created by hand and then later machine molded on stoneware. These crocks, churns, jugs, jars, plates, and pitchers were very important in the preparation and storage of foods and were necessary vessels in eighteenth- and nineteenth-century homes.

Although collectors will find that prices have soared in recent years, especially for decorated redware or stoneware with a rare design, there are less costly pieces still available. Unadorned redware and stoneware decorated with more common designs remain desirable and available for collecting.

Another type of earthenware that was created and became popular during the 1800s was yellowware. This pottery is still reasonably priced and collectors can build a desirable collection of these attractive kitchenware pieces.

During the late 1800s, when Victoriana was at its peak and nature was dis-played on everything from textiles to jewelry, a pottery called majolica became the rage. The naturalistic designs and soft pastel colors of this new pottery made it extremely popular from 1876 through the early 1900s. Today majolica is being sought by an ever-increasing number of collectors.

Numerous potteries began operation during the early 1900s and today collectors have taken great interest in these wares. Generally very affordable, collec-

Universal water jug with stopper, "Circus" pattern, 9″ tall, $48.00.

A yellowware teapot with basketweave design, 6″, which may have been used as a product premium, $125.00.

tors are finding merit in the kitchenware pieces produced by several Ohio potteries during the past century, including A.E. Hull Pottery, Nelson McCoy Pottery, Watt Pottery, Universal Potteries, and Harker Pottery.

Redware

Redware was the first pottery or earthenware to be made in America. The colonists found a red clay in the northeast and from it they created redware bowls, jars, jugs, molds, mugs, pie plates, pitchers, and occasional novelty items such as small figures and flowerpots.

Redware often was decorated with a slip-glaze design, which was a liquid containing ground clay, water, and lead. The slip glaze was used to coat soft redware pottery to help make it more durable, and during the process potters often indulged in a little creativity. Slip-glaze designs were simple swirls, flowers, stars, and wavy lines.

Colored glazes were made by adding certain minerals to the liquid clay mixture. For example, iron oxide made an orange glaze, manganese created black, and adding copper resulted in a green glaze.

Redware was produced by many small potteries until the 1850s when stoneware and yellowware were found to be more practical. Some of the early redware potters that had small shops in the east include John Bell (1830s), Waynesboro, Pennsylvania; Samuel and Solomon Bell (1850s), Strasburg, Virginia; the Brown Brothers (1860s), Huntington, New York; Rudolph Christ (early 1800s), Salem, North Carolina; Clark and Fox (1830s), Athens, New York; John Corliss (1850s), Woolrich, Maine; Fulper Pottery Company (late 1800s), Flemington, New Jersey; Morganville Pottery (1850 to 1900), Morganville, New York; and A. E. Smith (mid-1800s), Norwalk, Connecticut.

Small redware jug, circa 1860, 5" tall, $35.00.

Although redware was made into the nineteenth century, stoneware quickly replaced it. Stoneware was less expensive to produce and posed no health threat from lead poisoning.

Collectors will find that plain redware jugs and jars are available and affordable, but the more popular decorated pieces have become scarce. Those pieces decorated with a slip-glaze design can cost hundreds of dollars.

Stoneware

Utilitarian stoneware containers were being made by the early nineteenth century and were found to be more durable than redware. Stoneware was made from a mixture of gray clays and sand, and because it could be fired at extremely high temperatures, it was both hard and strong. However, potteries that produced the early gray stoneware were limited in the variety of pieces they could produce, because stoneware was not easily molded. The potters seemed to compensate by decorating their crocks, jugs, jars, churns, mugs, and pitchers with cobalt blue, black, or brown pictures, swirls, or numbers. Today collectors find that these simple

116

decorations will greatly influence both the desirability and price of stoneware pieces.

Very early pieces of stoneware were decorated by "slip-trailing": coloring through a design made in wet clay. Later on, freehand cobalt blue designs were painted on stoneware before firing, and by the late 1800s machine-made stoneware was produced with designs molded right into the surface.

Due to the fact that stoneware potters usually signed their work (and often inscribed a number on the piece to indicate gallon capacity), it is possible to attribute certain works to specific potteries. Well-known companies producing stoneware were located in New England, New York, Pennsylvania, Illinois, and Minnesota.

In 1793 Captain John Norton began Norton Potteries (synonymous with Bennington Pottery) in Bennington, Vermont, and initially produced redware pottery. With the discovery of the gray clays in New York and New Jersey, Norton turned his attention to stoneware and had the gray clay brought to Vermont by wagon. Norton Potteries produced the popular stoneware until the company closed in 1894, and it is noted for having produced a highly collectible array of decorated stoneware pieces.

Another highly collectible stoneware was produced by the Red Wing Stoneware Company (in the 1920s the name changed to Red Wing Union Stoneware Company) of Red Wing, Minnesota. Started in 1878 by David Hallum, the Red Wing Stoneware Company made stoneware in grays and browns with cobalt blue or black decorations.

After the turn of the century the stoneware was machine made with ma-

Six-gallon stoneware crock with black leaf and marked "Western Stoneware Co., Monmouth, Ill.," handles with black wooden knobs, 13" wide by 14" tall, $55.00.

chine-stamped designs. In 1912 Red Wing developed a red dye that could be used on their stoneware and they began stamping a red bird's wing on their wares.

The Red Wing Union Stoneware Company continued production until it closed in 1967, and it is considered one of the largest producers of stoneware in America.

Today collectors watch for early examples of Red Wing, such as crocks decorated with cobalt or black daisies, butterflies, leaves, and other designs.

Other companies recognized for having produced collectible stoneware include Cowden and Wilcox Pottery, Harrisburg, Pennsylvania; Hamilton and Pershing Pottery, Johnstown, Pennsylvania; Hamilton and Jones Pottery, Greensboro, Pennsylvania; John Bell Pottery, Waynesboro, Pennsylvania; Pfaltzgraff, York, Pennsylvania; Ottman Brothers, Fort Edward, New York; C.W. Braun, Buffalo, New York; N.A. White and Son, Utica, New York; and Peoria Pottery, Peoria, Illinois.

Collectors will note that early stone-

Stoneware butter churn, unmarked, 15" tall, $125.00.

ware pieces are the most sought after. It is the early examples that are heavily decorated and, therefore, most desirable. They now are considered a form of American folk art with their hand-drawn designs, and pieces depicting animals, farm scenes, birds, and houses have become rare, costing hundreds or thousands of dollars.

Stoneware decorated with swirls, flowers, and leaves is still available for collecting and can be found at antiques shows, auctions, and through antiques dealers who specialize in primitives and Americana. Plain stoneware often turns up at flea markets and auctions and is inexpensive to collect.

Stoneware pickle crock, brown lid marked "Pat. 3/1/92, The Weir, #5, April 16, 1901," 17″ tall, $125.00.

Yellowware pitcher with brown bands, 6¼″ tall, $25.00.

Rare European yellowware colander, 11″ wide, $230.00.

Yellowware

Yellowware pottery, so called because its clay turned a shade of yellow when fired (from buff to sunflower yellow and mustard), was extremely popular from the mid-nineteenth century through the 1930s.

Potteries located in New Jersey, Ohio, Maryland, and the New England states produced most of this practical earthenware. Notable potteries include the American Pottery Manufacturing Company, Salamander Works, International Pottery, and Lauton and Cory, all of New Jersey. Knowles, Taylor and Knowles Company; Industrial Pottery Works; C.C. Thompson Pottery Company; D.E. McNichol Pottery Company; and Star Pottery, located in Ohio and the Edwin Bennett Pottery of Maryland.

The pieces produced by these companies and others were usually unmarked and included sets of bowls, fruit jars, bean pots, jugs, teapots, molds, pie plates, dinner plates, rolling pins, colanders, custard cups, pitchers, chamber pots, foot warmers, and the occasional novelty item.

By the late 1800s yellowware could be purchased through mail-order catalogs and the sets of nesting bowls were very popular. This utilitarian pottery saw widespread use and production during the late 1800s and continued to be made into the 1930s, competing with other popular wares.

Today collectors find yellowware still is readily available, and there are several

Yellowware bowl with brown and white bands, 12" size, $55.00.

Nest of three yellowware bowls with brown bands, 7", 8", and 9", $45.00 for set.

Rare yellowware rolling pin, 15" long, $450.00.

types to look for. Very early yellowware was made quite plain with no decoration of any kind. Decorated yellowware became popular by the mid-nineteenth century and was made with bands of color (white, brown, blue, and green) on the bowls, pitchers, jars, and so forth. Rockingham-glazed yellowware also was made from the 1850s through the 1870s and had a mottled brown appearance. By the late 1800s, molded yellowware was being produced and a wide assortment of designs decorated this popular pottery, especially the yellowware produced between the early 1900s and the 1930s.

Some of the more common pieces found today include bowls, custard cups, and pie plates whereas pieces such as

Small Rockingham bowl, 5", $35.00.

pitchers, fruit jars, rolling pins, and washboards have become rare.

Majolica floral and three-leaf plate, 9", $65.00.

Majolica

Majolica, a colorful pottery of the Victorian era, has seen renewed interest and popularity among antiques enthusiasts and collectors.

Late nineteenth-century majolica derived its name from a pottery made hundreds of years ago on the small Mediterranean island of Majorca. Initially the Italians imported earthenware from Majorca and began producing a majolica pottery. This early majolica did not resemble the majolica that collectors seek today. The name was passed on and during the seventeenth century when a Frenchman named Bernard Palissy made a pottery decorated with nature designs, it, too, was called majolica. It was Palissy's work that influenced the design of the majolica made during the late nineteenth century.

Minton and Company of England exhibited a colorful new earthenware at London's Great Exhibition in 1851. This "new" majolica was an immediate success and other English firms began production. Twenty-five years after London's Great Exhibition, majolica was displayed in the United States at the 1876 Philadelphia Centennial Exhibition by the

Floral majolica luncheon plate, 7" size, $40.00.

English potteries of Palissy, Whieldon, Wedgwood, and Holdcroft.

It was not long before several American companies became known for their production of this pottery that often depicted vegetables, leaves, and flowers in shades of deep brown, soft pink, pastel greens, blues, and lavender. The American manufacturers included the Edwin Bennett Pottery, Baltimore, Maryland; Chesapeake Pottery Company, Baltimore, Maryland; Wannopee Pottery Company, New Milford, Connecticut; Charles Reynolds, Trenton, New Jersey; Morley and Company, Wellsville, Ohio;

121

Bamboo and Bow majolica platter, 13″ long, $145.00.

Leaf-on-Leaf platter, 12″ long, $95.00.

Griffen, Smith, and Hill, Phoenixville, Pennsylvania (which is noted for creating the highly collectible shell and seaweed motif); Faience Manufacturing Company, Greenpoint, New York; and the Hampshire Pottery Company, Keene, New Hampshire.

Although almost all of the English-made majolica was marked, most of this pottery that was made in the United States was not. Collectors often must study the credits of the various American manufacturers to identify makers. For exam-

ple, both the Wannopee Pottery Company and Charles Reynolds made tea sets and dinnerware in the popular lettuce leaf design.

While majolica enjoyed popularity because of its colorful designs, it also was successful because it was inexpensive. Majolica was even used as a product premium for the customers of A&P grocery stores with the purchase of various items.

Today majolica enthusiasts usually collect according to item, theme, or the pottery. Popular items for building a col-

Majolica leaf plate, 7", $38.00.

lection include majolica baskets, bowls, pieces with covers (such as butter dishes), mugs, pitchers, plates, oyster plates, platters, tea sets, or novelty items such as vases or figurals. Common themes for building a collection include corn, begonias, shells, bamboo, animals, birds, fruit, and vegetables.

Majolica still is available for collecting and can be found at antiques shows and shops, pottery shows, and auctions. While not inexpensive, collectors still can build a desirable collection of majolica pieces by studying the various potteries and examining pieces closely to determine the quality of the workmanship and the condition of the piece.

Collectible Twentieth-Century Pottery

During the late nineteenth century and the early 1900s, numerous potteries sprang into operation, many of them located in Ohio and Virginia. Several of these companies produced kitchenware and tableware lines that have become popular among collectors.

A.E. HULL POTTERY

The Red Riding Hood line of kitchenware items produced between 1943 and

Little Red Riding Hood cookie jar, 13", $100.00.

Red Riding Hood pitcher, marked "PAT." on the bottom, 8", $125.00.

1957 by the A.E. Hull Pottery Company are highly collectible. Hull Pottery of Zanesville, Ohio, was established in 1905 and produced stoneware, art ware, novelties, and kitchenware until the company closed in 1986.

Red Riding Hood salt and pepper, 3¼", the pair $27.00.

Along with their popular Red Riding Hood line, Hull also produced early kitchenware in solid colors, often with contrasting bands of color. A kitchenware line called Cinderella was introduced in 1948, and a line called Sunglow was offered in the 1950s.

These kitchenware lines usually include such pieces as bowls, casseroles, pitchers, salt and peppers, sugars and creamers, teapots, and cookie jars.

With the exception of rare and costly Red Riding Hood pieces (such as canisters and biscuit jars), Hull pottery is still affordable, but prices are on the rise.

McCoy Pottery

McCoy Pottery, known among collectors for their production of collectible cookie jars, was established in Roseville, Ohio, in 1910. At that time it was known as the Nelson McCoy Sanitary Stoneware Company and offered customers a wide assortment of items such as crocks, churns, and jars.

During the 1930s the company became known as the Nelson McCoy Pottery Company, and they continued their production of stoneware, turning out a popular blue and white line along with glossy brown stoneware items. By the 1940s the company turned its attention to specialty items, tablewares, and the

McCoy Frontier Town cookie jar (unmarked), 10" tall, $42.00.

McCoy Honey Bear cookie jar, 8" tall, $70.00.

numerous cookie jars collectors seek today.

Prices are reasonable for McCoy cookie jars (most are priced between $35.00 and $100.00) with the exception of several rare cookie jars such as Two Kittens in a Basket, Tan Kangaroo, Indian Head, Caboose, Christmas Tree, and Davy Crockett.

Watt "Ovenware 07 USA," bowl, cherry pattern, 7½", $20.00.

McCoy Black Mammie cookie jar, 11" tall, $150.00.

Watt pitcher, cherry pattern, circa 1950s, 5½" tall, $30.00.

Watt "Ovenware 76" pot, cherry pattern, 6" tall, $30.00.

WATT POTTERY

Established in Crooksville, Ohio, in 1922, the Watt Pottery Company was responsible for producing the Red Apple kitchenware and dinnerware line that collectors seek today.

Watt Pottery also produced several other lines, including Rooster, Basket Weave, Morning Glory, Red Tulip, Blue Tulip, Wood Grain, Pennsylvania Dutch

Universal Calico Fruit divided
plate, 9″, $10.00.

Universal covered refrigerator jug, 7″ tall, $38.00.

Universal Cat Tail divided plate, 9″, $15.00.

Tulip, and Star Flower until fire closed
the company in 1965.

All these attractive designs decorated a wide assortment of hand-painted
kitchenware and ovenware pieces that
collectors are finding more prominently
displayed at antiques shows. With the exception of hard-to-find Red Apple pieces,
most Watt pottery is very affordable.

UNIVERSAL POTTERIES

Another Ohio company, Universal
Potteries Incorporated, located in Cam-

bridge, produced only limited amounts
of dinnerware but also made numerous
collectible kitchenware items between
1934 and 1956. Universal's wares included bowls, water jugs with stoppers,
pie plates, platters, sugars and creamers,
casserole dishes, mixing bowls, and other
assorted items.

Universal's wares were produced in
several shapes, including Ballerina and
Upico, and were decorated with attractive decals resulting in several popular
lines such as Calico Fruit (which was sold
through Montgomery Ward and other de-

126

Universal Cat Tail pattern on coffee percolator, 13½" tall, $165.00.

Harker bowl marked "Harker Hot Oven China-ware," Mallow pattern, 9", $12.50.

Universal salt and pepper, 4½", the pair $5.00.

partment stores), Hollyhock, Circus, Red Poppy, Iris, Rambler Rose, and Cat Tail (which was made for Sears, Roebuck and Company from 1934 to 1956).

A 1940 Sears catalog offered Cat Tail ovenproof kitchenware, "each piece fully guaranteed oven-proof and acid-proof—will be replaced if it crazes in baking." A three-piece casserole set (casserole dish,

lid, and plate) cost $1.19. Other kitchenware items were available, such as the deep-dish pie plate (bake and serve), which sold for $0.57.

Collectors should note that Universal's water jugs are a popular kitchenware item today but should have the stopper to be of real value.

HARKER POTTERY

Harker Pottery was established in East Liverpool, Ohio, in 1840 by Benjamin Harker. The company's early wares included yellowware and whiteware, and after the turn of the century they produced dinnerware.

The plant was relocated to Chester, West Virginia, in 1931, and they continued production of dinnerware lines and Hotoven kitchenware items, which were decorated with decals. In the late 1930s Harker introduced Cameoware.

Some of Harker's more popular decal-decorated lines include English Countryside, Rosebud, Fruits, Mallow, Petit Point Rose, Deco-Dahlia, Cottage, Red Apple, and Colonial Lady.

Kitchenware and the Hotoven lines included such pieces as pitchers, salt and peppers, bowls, waffle sets, servers, rolling pins, bean pots, covered casseroles, sugar and creamers, three-bowl stacking sets, teapots, custard cups, and lard jars with covers.

Rare Harker Colonial Lady teapot, 10″, $75.00.

Harker Cameoware covered casserole, pink, $8.00.

Harker Calico Tulip eggcup, 4½″, $5.00.

Harker Cameoware coffeepot, blue, 9″ tall, $28.00.

Cameoware was available in blue, pink, and yellow and was also sold by Montgomery Ward under the name Carv-Kraft.

The Harker Pottery Company was sold to Jeanette Glass in 1972.

Look for Harker Pottery pieces to turn up at flea markets, house and yard sales, and now antiques shops and shows. Harker kitchenware items are plentiful and offer collectors the opportunity to build a collection for a very small investment.

CHAPTER 8 Storage Containers in the Kitchen

Coffee.

For the collector interested in old kitchenware items, containers used in the gathering and storing of food and staples provide several different areas of collecting. There are those who collect baskets, Victorian china "cereal sets," wooden spice cupboards, fruit jars, enameled tinware canisters, refrigerator containers, and even plastics.

Kitchen glassware has become quite popular among collectors. What can be more nostalgic than an old Hoosier kitchen cabinet complete with glass canisters, spice jars, and saltbox? Today these items are eagerly sought and collectors are paying rising prices to add to their collections.

Flea markets, house sales, and auctions offer vintage 1940 to 1950 plastic canister sets and accessories that are quickly drawing the interest of collectors. These modernistic wares will continue to draw attention as they become one of the newly discovered collectibles of the 1990s.

The wide assortment of containers used in the kitchen brings diversity in texture, variations in color, and an assortment of shapes to any collection of old kitchenware.

Baskets

Baskets have been used for centuries as receptacles for foodstuffs. They were made by hand until the late 1800s when the Industrial Revolution introduced machinery for basketmaking.

Various materials (often specific to a particular region) have been used in basketmaking, but most of the baskets collectors find today are made of splint, straw, or willow.

For example, baskets used for collecting berries were originally made by shaving splints from wet logs of oak or hickory, and then weaving them in an over-and-under pattern. By 1880 machines were able to cut splint in a uniform size. Round and oval egg baskets, popular along the East Coast, were made by sewing strips of straw, coiling them, and then binding the coils together. During the late Victorian era willow baskets of various sizes were made and often were used to display fresh fruit.

Today collectors search for the more desirable handmade (pre-1880) baskets rather than the machine-made ones. Interested collectors should learn to recognize signs of age and wear (such as

French enamelware canister set, red with white flower and leaf design, sucre 6″, farine 5½″, cafe 5″, and thé 4″, the set is $275.00.

Large market basket, 18″ long, $35.00.

Splint basket with side handles, 14″ long by 7½″ tall, $48.00.

Miniature melon basket, 3¼″ high by 5¼″ wide, $145.00.

darkened colors and faded paint) to be certain a basket is truly old, as many skilled artisans continue to hand-craft new baskets today.

Fruit Jars

Home canning became popular in 1858 with the advent of John Mason's patented zinc screw cap and rubber ring for canning jars. The convenience and ease in using this lid prompted an increase in production of jars as more and more

Oak splint basket with handle, 12″ long by 4″ high, $65.00

Mason Improved canning jar, aqua blue, 7″ tall, $15.00.

"Atlas Improved Mason" jar, aqua blue, 7″ tall, $7.00.

women found it practical to can for home use.

Most canning jars were an aqua color or clear glass. Limited amounts were produced in cobalt blue, black, or amber and these are quite rare today.

The turn of the century brought about more modern means of producing glass jars and also saw the invention of the lid that is still used today—the one developed then for the Economy Jar. Julius Landsberger developed the Economy Jar in 1903; the flat, metal lid has a coating

Unusual French canning jar, green with thistle design, marked "LaLorraine 1 Liter," circa 1930, 9" tall, $58.00.

"The Ideal" canning jar, aqua blue, 7" tall, $16.00.

on the underside that makes it fasten to the jar.

An early 1900 booklet published by the Hazel-Atlas Glass Company of Wheeling, West Virginia, stated, "The first machine-made fruit jars were produced by the Hazel-Atlas Glass Company. Atlas Jars, being machine made, are therefore uniform in size, shape and appearance. . . . All Atlas Jars are made of Clear Crystal [flint] glass, of highest quality, giving the natural color to packed fruits or vegetables."

Hazel-Atlas Glass Company offered four different styles of fruit jar, including the Atlas Good Luck square jars, "Recommended to those who desire a jar for fancy packs or exhibit purposes"; the Atlas Mason square jars, "Recommended to those who take particular pride in the appearance of their preserves"; the Atlas E-Z Seal jar, an all-glass, sanitary package; and the Atlas Mason Strong Shoulder jar that "has been on the market for

over fifty years but has been improved by the Strong Shoulder feature."

There are thousands of canning jars available for collecting. Interested collectors can find other familiar names, including Ball, Canton, Ideal, Mason, Lightning, Peerless, Wears, Woodbury, Crown, and Putnam. Collectors should consider the age and color of a jar and whether it has any special markings. Prices can range from just a few dollars to hundreds of dollars for a rare example.

Spice Cupboards and Boxes

During the eighteenth and early nineteenth centuries spices were a precious and valuable commodity in the United States. Wooden spice cupboards, which could be locked, protected these herbs and spices.

Even after increased travel and trade

Small spice cupboard, six drawers, all original, 8″ high by 7″ wide, $195.00.

Seven-drawer spice cupboard with porcelain knobs, tiger maple wood, 15″ high by 9″ wide, $325.00.

Unusual tramp art spice cupboard, black with gold trim, 13½″ high by 9½″ wide, $295.00.

with other countries made spices more readily available, the spice cupboard still remained popular. These small hand-crafted cupboards often had several drawers to hold an assortment of spices, and the entire unit usually was hung on a wall.

Spice boxes also were used during the same period and often were made of japanned tin or wood. Spice box sets could be purchased with six or more small containers housed in one large round or square box.

Japanned Tin Canisters

During the late eighteenth and early nineteenth centuries wooden boxes (see Chapter 9, Pantry Boxes), and stoneware crocks were used to store staples such as flour and sugar. As industrialization increased in the second half of the nineteenth century, smaller canisters were made of tin-lined brass or copper, and later japanned tin.

Japanned tin canisters, spice sets, match holders, and round cheese or cracker boxes were very popular during the Victorian era. Before they could be purchased through the mail-order catalogs and at local emporiums, these con-

Early wooden spice box with lid, eight spice containers, 9¼" wide by 3½" high, $325.00.

Japanned tin canister set, coffee 7", tea 5½", and box containing six 2½" spice tins, the set is $75.00.

Matchbox holder, black with floral decoration, 6" high by 3" wide, $8.00.

Blue-green round spice tin with six spice containers for nutmeg, mace, cloves, cinnamon, allspice, and ginger, 7¼" wide by 3¼" high, $115.00.

tainers were sold door to door by peddlers.

The 1902 Sears Roebuck catalog offered imported European japanned tinware with lithographed decorations. A spice box with six round spice containers sold for $0.48; a round, decorated 1-pound-size coffee canister with a porcelain knob was $0.10; and the 2-pound size was $0.12.

Pottery Canisters

Pottery canister sets also became popular during the late Victorian era and these lovely, fragile (they chipped easily) containers often had hand-painted decorations.

By 1900 imported German and

From a turn-of-the-century Czechoslovakian cereal set, a flour, salt, and rice canister, eight-piece set $95.00.

From the same set as the previous photo, the tea, coffee, and sugar canisters, eight-piece set $95.00.

Blue and white coffee canister marked "Made in Germany," early 1900s, 7" high, $59.00.

Czechoslovakian sets were being sold in the United States, where they often were referred to as cereal sets. An early Sears Roebuck catalog offered a German cereal and spice set made of heavily glazed china with flow-blue decorations. This thir-teen-piece set included six cereal jars (oatmeal, rice, prunes, sugar, coffee, and tea), six spice jars (cloves, cinnamon, pepper, nutmeg, allspice, and ginger), and a saltbox with a hardwood cover. In 1908 Sears Roebuck sold this complete set for $2.69.

The saltbox that was sold as a part of the cereal and spice set was an important kitchenware item because salt was necessary for seasoning meats and vegetables as they cooked.

Many of these imported cereal sets have only the name of the country in which they were made stamped on the bottom of each piece. Collectors can easily determine if a set was made in Germany, Czechoslovakia, or Japan. Collectors also find that many of these sets included oil and vinegar cruets with china or cork stoppers.

Although complete sets in excellent condition are rare, they do turn up at antiques shows or auctions and collectors

Vinegar and oil pitchers, marked "Made in Germany," 7" tall, the pair $15.00.

Saltbox, white with blue lettering and wooden top, 6¼" high by 5½" wide, $60.00.

Green depression glass cookie jar with screw-on lid, 8" high by 6" wide, $38.00.

will pay hundreds of dollars for such a find. Individual pieces and partial sets can be collected for very little cost but most pieces may have small chips or cracks from constant use. Canister lids are especially prone to cracks and chips, because these were handled most often.

Glass Canisters

During the early 1900s glass canister sets were produced and often were included with the purchase of the popular hoosier-style kitchen cabinet. Many of these kitchen cabinets had glass sugar dispensers, glass spice jars, coffee and tea containers in assorted sizes, and glass saltboxes.

The many companies noted for producing depression glass dinnerware also made a wide array of kitchenware. These companies include Hazel-Atlas Glass Company, Jeannette Glass Company,

Coffee and flour canisters with rare push-on lids, green jadite, 7¼" tall, each $75.00.

Glass containers. Spice, 4½", $5.00; salt, 4½" tall, $10.00; tea, 5" tall by 3½" wide, $12.00.

McKee, Hocking Glass Company, U.S. Glass, and the Sneath Company. Their glass kitchenware items included canisters, saltboxes, salt and pepper shakers, sugar shakers, refrigerator containers, and numerous other items.

This glass kitchenware was first made of crystal (clear) glass; by the 1920s it came in several popular colors, including blue (transparent, opaque, and delphite), amber, black, custard, clambroth (a translucent off-white), green (both transparent and opaque jadite), white, yellow (transparent and opaque Seville), pink, and red (transparent and fired on).

While much of the colored glassware is scarce today, many items are readily

Glass flour (white) and sugar (black) shakers, 5" tall, each $12.00.

Glass salt and pepper shakers with black screw-on lids, late 1940s, "Tappan" on chef's hat, yellow, 3½", pair $12.00.

Square cake box, enameled tin, blue with flower-pot decorations and glass knob, 10" wide by 4½" high, $17.00.

available for collecting. For example, kitchenware in cobalt blue by the Hazel-Atlas Company is very rare, and therefore, expensive, whereas crystal, opaque custard, and transparent green are still available and reasonably priced. Collectors can consider themselves fortunate if they have a matched set (canisters, spice jars, and saltbox).

Glass kitchenware can be found at antiques shops and shows and at glassware shows. Odd pieces often turn up at flea markets and house sales and persevering collectors often can acquire a collection by building on a series of finds.

Enameled Tinware Containers

Enameled bread tin, red and white, 10" high, $4.00.

While pottery and glassware canisters and accessories remained popular through the 1930s, enameled tinware sets were also being manufactured. For example, the 1924 Montgomery Ward catalog offered a six-piece spice set made of ivory colored enameled tin and decorated with light blue Dutch windmill scenes. The six-piece set was priced $0.79.

The National Enameling and Stamping Company (NESCO) sold canister sets and other kitchen items in solid colors with a trim—such as ivory with green trim and white with blue trim. Three of NESCO's popular lines during the 1930s included Country Girl, Garden Girl, and Delphinium. Each line was known by a specific color combination with a cheerful decal depicting scenes such as a country girl or garden girl. The enamelware kitchen containers and accessories remained popular during the 1940s, but

Green speckled enameled tin bread box with decal, 15″ wide by 10″ high, $15.00.

Enameled tin canister set, white with red lid and tulip design, marked "Decorator" on canister bottom, sizes 5″, 6″, 7″, and 8″, the set is $27.50.

were given stiff competition by new, modern plastic kitchenwares.

Plastic Containers

The colorful, modernistic kitchen of the late 1940s was being accessorized with plastic. For example, Tupperware, developed by Earl S. Tupper of Farnumsville, Massachusetts, was growing popular by the late 1940s. Covered bowls, refrigerator sets, and canisters were just a few of their products. In 1946 Tupperware was first sold by way of the home party, and because this proved to be such a success, Tupperware Home Parties Inc. was formed in 1951.

Other popular plastic wares were produced by Columbus Plastic Products of Columbus, Ohio. Their Lustro Ware line was a good seller, and during the late 1940s a four-piece canister set, available in red or yellow, sold for $3.49.

After World War II several other companies concentrated on producing plastic kitchenwares, and today we find that these items from the 1940s and 1950s are beginning to turn up at flea markets, house and yard sales, and secondhand shops. They cost very little to collect.

Red and white plastic Lustro Ware bread box, 18″ long, $1.00.

Large square covered refrigerator container, yellow glass, 8½″ by 3½″ high, $25.00.

Kitchen Kraft refrigerator container, part of a three-piece stacking set, the set is $125.00.

Refrigerator Containers

The Hall China Company of East Liverpool, Ohio, produced several lines of refrigerator ware during the 1930s and 1940s, including Aristocrat, Bingo, Emperor, Norris, Patrician, and Plaza. Some of Hall's refrigerator wares were made specifically for an appliance manufacturer while others could be bought at the department store. The items produced included water jugs, servers, and covered leftover dishes. These wares were often included with the purchase of a new refrigerator.

The 1932 *Silent Hostess Treasure Book*, an advertising cookbook offered by General Electric Company, included information that helped readers make the greatest use of their GE refrigerators. It included (along with recipes, menu planning, and so forth) a section on refrigerator accessories. Accessories that could be purchased from a General Electric dealer included glass refrigerator dishes, sanitary porcelain refrigerator bowls, and water bottles. The glass refrigerator dishes were available in a square or oblong shape, as a single unit or in sets, and could be used in the oven as well as in the refrigerator. The sanitary refrigerator bowls

Fire King refrigerator-to-oven containers, large, 9″ long, $25.00; small, 4″, $8.50.

Green jadite water container, 11″ long by 4½″ high, $150.00.

Kitchen Kraft pie plate and server, 9½″ plate, $25.00.

were sold with flat lids for stacking and were available in ivory, green, and rose porcelain.

Water bottles with a metal cap "can keep you supplied with pure, cold drinking water . . . especially designed to fit alongside the Super-freezer to use a min-imum of space," according to the GE *Silent Hostess Treasure Book*.

Many of the companies that produced glass kitchenwares also manufactured refrigerator accessories in transparent and opaque colors, such as Jeannette Glass Company, McKee Glass Company, Hazel-

Kitchen Kraft utility bowl with Oriental decoration, 10″, $35.00.

Kitchen Kraft green utility bowl, 10″, $65.00.

Atlas Glass Company, and Hocking Glass Company.

For example, in the June 1942 *Ladies' Home Journal*, the Indiana Glass Company of Dunkirk, Indiana, advertised their refrigerator Kontanerettes and Conserv-O-Jars, which could be placed on a revolving tray. Both styles were pie shaped, transparent glass, and available in different sizes. The Kontanerettes were sold as a three-jar set for $0.85, a four-jar set for $1.00, a five-jar set for $2.50, and a large, six-jar set for $3.50.

Many well-known potteries also included refrigerator containers among the kitchenware items they produced. For example, the Homer Laughlin China Company of Newell, West Virginia, produced Kitchen Kraft items from 1937 through the 1940s in the popular Fiesta ware colors; some pieces were decorated with decals.

Although glass and pottery refrigerator containers and accessories continued to be sold through the 1940s, plastic took over during the next decade and became the big seller.

CHAPTER 9 Woodenware

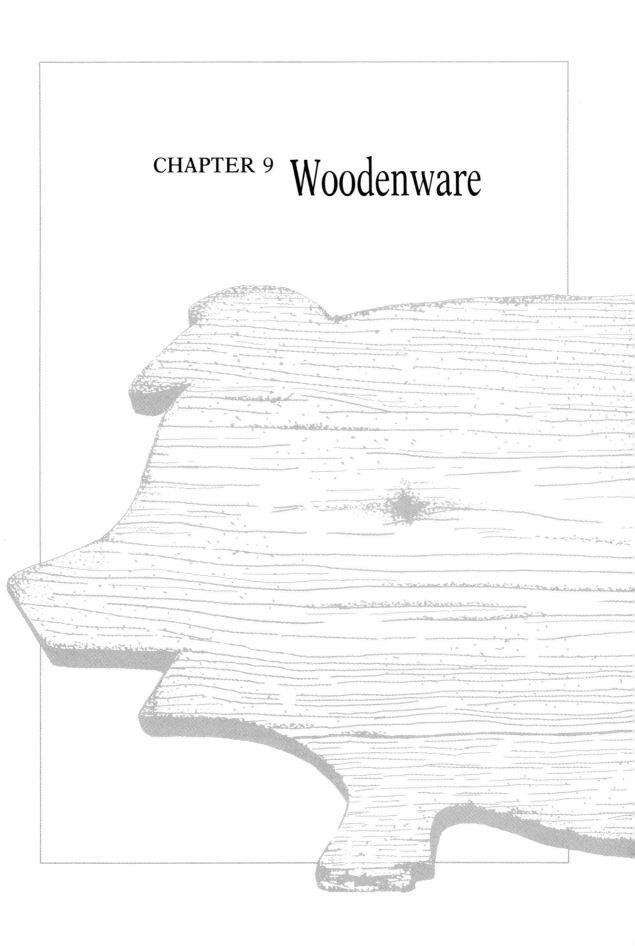

Woodenware items—also called "treenware" from the word *tree*—are considered primitives. They were the seventeenth-, eighteenth-, and nineteenth-century vessels and tools of food preparation.

Woodenware in America was first made by European coopers. *Cooper* was the trade name given to men who handcrafted the everyday wooden items with the help of a lathe.

During the nineteenth century, progress and the advent of the Industrial Revolution introduced machine-powered lathes that could then complete the work of the cooper. As a result, woodenware items were factory made in large numbers.

Assorted woodenware items still found today include bowls, breadboards, dough boxes, candle boxes, spoons, butter molds, sugar firkins, pantry boxes, knife boxes, and butter churns. Burl bowls and Shaker pantry boxes are rare and cost hundreds of dollars, as do other early hand-crafted examples. As a result, collectors find merit and more affordable prices in the nineteenth-century machine-made woodenware.

A collection of woodenware lends a

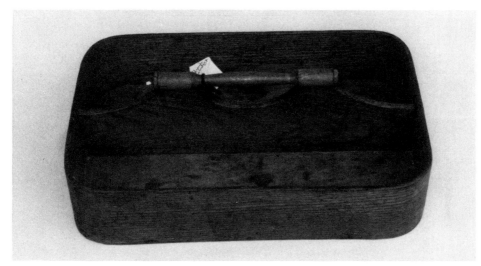

Wooden cutlery box, 13″ long by 8½″ wide, $135.00.

Rare and large burl dipper,
18″ long by 6″ deep, $325.00.

Rare handmade wooden blueberry rake with metal tines, 9″ long, $125.00.

Small cutting board, 7″ long, $25.00.

colonial or country feel to a modern-day kitchen, and many of these pieces can be used if the wood is treated properly.

Collectors find woodenware at antiques shows and shops, and especially through dealers who specialize in primitives. Anyone interested in collecting woodenware should be aware that these items are still being made today and can achieve an "aged" look very quickly through constant use.

Breadboards

Round or oblong wooden breadboards were used during the eighteenth and nineteenth centuries for slicing and serving fresh home-baked bread. Occasionally these boards were decorated with a hand-carved prayer or inspirational message, but most were quite plain.

During the late Victorian era, when patterned glassware became popular, the wooden breadboard was put aside in favor of this more formal glass platter for serving bread.

By the turn of the century, machine-made wooden breadboards once again

were being used and became a standard pull-out feature on the popular hoosier-type kitchen cabinets.

Wooden Bowls

Woodenware bowls were made for food preparation and eating. Most wooden bowls were made of maple, elm, chestnut, or ash. Woodenware bowls remain available for collecting today and cost considerably less than burl bowls. Collectors may occasionally find traces of paint on the outside of old wooden bowls. The bowls often were painted to help preserve the wood and add a dash of color to an otherwise plain kitchen.

Round breadboard with carved leaf design, 11″ across, matching bread knife, the set is $95.00.

Pig cutting board, 18″ long, $30.00.

Wooden bowl, 11″, $20.00.

Maple wood bowl, 17½″ long by 9¼″ wide, $135.00.

"White Cedar Cylinder Churn, Made in U.S.A.," 3-gallon capacity, 16″ tall by 15″ wide, $115.00.

Butter Churns and Molds

BUTTER CHURNS

During the seventeenth, eighteenth, and early nineteenth centuries butter making was a tedious task that was usually assigned to the children of the household. Little hands would work nonstop at churning the milk into butter.

Early butter churns were made in a barrel shape with a plunger mechanism.

By the nineteenth century a crank handle for churning had made the job somewhat easier.

After the churning process was complete, the butter was squeezed to remove liquids and then packed into tubs.

BUTTER MOLDS

Small round or rectangular molds were used to decorate, identify, and advertise butter. Introduced into the United States by Swiss settlers, butter molds were first hand-carved at home and then later made by the local cooper.

Wooden butter churn, 18" tall, $139.00.

Dovetailed rectangular butter mold with two star designs, 6" wide, $37.00.

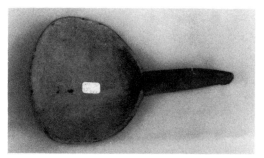

Wooden butter paddle, 9" long, $24.00.

Butter mold with acorn and leaf design, 4", $145.00.

Butter mold, leaf design, 4" size, $75.00.

Flowers, hearts, thistles, animals, stars, and fruit are just a few examples of the decorations carved into these hardwood molds. Other molds had a family name or a special symbol to identify the farm the butter came from.

As with other woodenware items, the butter mold was being machine cut by the late 1800s and was made of aluminum by the turn of the century.

Today collectors find that certain molds are considered rare (such as birds

Round pantry box with lid, 8¼″ wide by 4″ high, $59.00.

Small wooden cheese box, 5½″ wide, $24.00.

Pantry box, oval with original blue paint, 8½″ long by 4″ high, $150.00.

Small pantry box with original mustard paint, 5″ wide by 2½″ high, $85.00.

and animals) and, therefore, can cost hundreds of dollars whereas more common designs (flowers and fruit) can still be found a more modest prices. These collectibles are considered by many to be a form of early folk art and they are often desirable for the piece of Americana they represent.

Pantry Boxes

Utilitarian, wooden pantry boxes were used to store kitchen staples. They were usually made at home by men who crafted the round boxes from steamed strips of wood, carved thin with a pointed lap. Craftsmen would use whatever wood was available—usually pine, oak, maple, chestnut, or birch— and often would make a set of boxes graduating in size to fit one within the other. These pantry boxes, from small to large, also were known as nesting boxes.

The smaller pantry boxes held pills and popular spices such as cinnamon, nutmeg, pepper, and ginger. Other boxes were made in different sizes to store meal, cheese, butter, herbs, and pies. Some pantry boxes were decorated with a design on the lid or the entire box might have been painted some shade of gray, green, yellow, or blue.

The Shaker communities handcrafted oval pantry boxes. Their boxes were constructed using copper tacks and most often were made in sets of twelve. Shaker-made pantry boxes are very rare, costing hundreds of dollars.

Bibliography

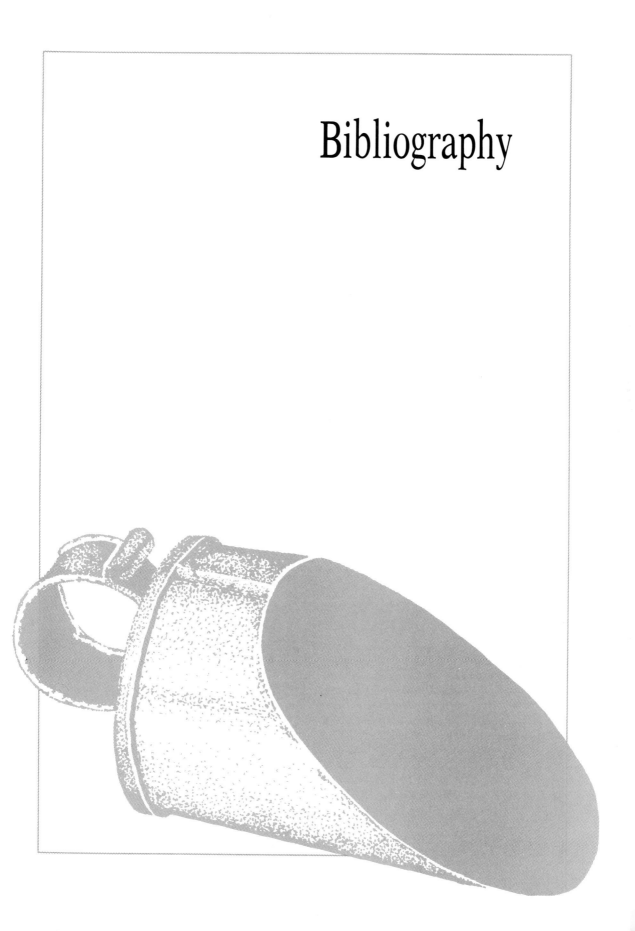

Books

Noted at the end of each entry (in parentheses) are the sections in this book for which the entry may add additional information.

Beecher, Catherine E., and Harriet Beecher Stowe. *The American Woman's Home.* Hartford, Conn.: The Stowe-Day Foundation, 1987. (Introduction.)

Beeton, Isabella. *Beeton's Book of Household Management,* facsimile ed. New York: Farrar, Straus, and Giroux, 1969. (Introduction.)

Bergevin, Al. *Food and Drink Containers and Their Prices.* Radnor, Pa.: Wallace-Homestead Book Company, 1987. (Chapters 1 and 8.)

Better Homes and Gardens. Living the Country Life. Des Moines, Iowa: Meredith Corporation, 1986. (Chapters 3, 4, 5, 7, and 9.)

Celehar, Jane H. *Kitchens and Gadgets—1920 to 1950.* Radnor, Pa.: Wallace-Homestead Book Company, 1982. (Introduction; Chapters 2, 5, and 8.)

———. *Kitchens and Kitchenware—1900 to 1950.* Lombard, Ill.: Wallace-Homestead Book Company, 1985. (Introduction; Chapters 1, 2, 3, 5, 6, 8, and 9.)

Cole, Brian. *Boxes.* Radnor, Pa.: Chilton Book Company, 1976. (Chapter 8.)

Cunningham, Jo. *The Collector's Encyclopedia of American Dinnerware.* Paducah, Ky.: Collector Books, 1989. (Chapters 4 and 8.)

Duke, Harvey. *Official Identification and Price Guide to Pottery and Porcelain,* seventh ed. New York: The House of Collectibles, 1989. (Chapters 4 and 8.)

Farmer, Fannie Merritt. *The Boston Cooking School Cook Book.* Boston: Little, Brown, and Company, 1933. (Introduction and Chapter 5.)

Fisher, C. *Hazelcorn's Price Guide to Old Electric Toasters.* Teaneck, N.J.: H.J.H. Publications. (Chapter 2.)

Florence, Gene. *The Collector's Encyclopedia of Depression Glass,* seventh ed. Paducah, Ky.: Collector Books, 1986. (Chapter 4.)

———. *Kitchen Glassware of the Depression Years,* third ed. Paducah, Ky.: Collector Books, 1987. (Chapters 1 and 8.)

Franklin, Linda Campbell. *300 Years of Kitchen Collectibles,* second ed. Florence, Ala.: Books Americana, Inc., 1984. (Chapters 1, 2, 3, 5, 8, and 9.)

Fredgant, Don. *American Manufactured Furniture.* West Chester, Pa.: Schiffer Publishing Ltd., 1988. (Chapter 6.)

———. *Electrical Collectibles.* San Luis Obispo, Calif.: Padre Productions, 1981. (Introduction and Chapter 2.)

Friday, Franklin. *A Walk Through the Park.* Louisville, Ky.: Elfun Historical Society, 1987. (Chapter 2.)

Gilliatt, Mary. *English Country Style.* Boston: Little, Brown, and Company, 1986. (Introduction and Chapter 5.)

Greguire, Helen. *The Collector's Encyclopedia of Graniteware.* Paducah, Ky.: Collector Books, 1990. (Chapter 3.)

Harned, Bill, and Denise Harned. *Griswold Cast Collectibles—History and Value,* seventh printing. Elmwood, Conn.: PRS-Harned, 1989. (Chapters 2, 3, and 5.)

Huxford, Sharon, and Bob Huxford. *The Collector's Encyclopedia of Fiesta with Harlequin and Riviera,* sixth ed. Paducah, Ky.: Collector Books, 1987. (Chapters 4 and 8.)

———. *Schroeder's Antiques Price Guide.* Paducah, Ky.: Collector Books, 1990. (Chapters 1, 3, 4, 5, 7, 8, and 9.)

Johnson, Frances. *Wallace-Homestead Price Guide to Baskets,* second ed. Radnor,

Pa.: Wallace-Homestead Book Company, n.d. (Chapter 8.)

Jones, Joseph Jr. *American Ice Boxes.* Humble, Tex.: Jobeco Books, 1981. (Chapter 2.)

Kennedy, Philip D. *Hoosier Cabinets.* Philip D. Kennedy, 9256 Holyoke Court, Indianapolis, Ind., 1989. (Chapter 6.)

Ketchum, William Jr. *The Catalog of American Antiques.* New York: Rutledge Books, 1979. (Introduction; Chapters 1, 2, 3, 5, 7, 8, and 9.)

Kovel, Ralph, and Terry Kovel. *Know Your Collectibles.* New York: Crown Publishers, Inc., 1981. (Chapters 1, 3, 5, 7, and 9.)

Lantz, Louise K. *Old American Kitchenware 1725–1925.* Hanover, Pa.: Everybody's Press, 1970. (Introduction; Chapters 2, 3, 5, 7, 8, and 9.)

Leibowitz, Joan. *Yellow Ware—The Transitional Ceramic.* West Chester, Pa.: Schiffer Publishing Ltd., 1985. (Chapters 5 and 7.)

Leopold, Allison Kyle. *Victorian Splendor.* New York: Stewart, Tabori and Chang, Inc., 1986. (Introduction.)

Lifshey, Earl. *The Housewares Story.* Chicago: National Housewares Manufacturers Association, 1973. (Chapters 2, 3, 5, and 8.)

Mace, O. Henry. *Collector's Guide to Victoriana.* Radnor, Pa.: Wallace-Homestead Book Company, 1991. (Introduction and Chapter 5.)

Marks, Mariann. *Majolica Pottery.* Paducah, Ky.: Collector Books, 1983. (Chapter 7.)

Marshall, Jo. *Kitchenware.* Radnor, Pa.: Chilton Book Company, 1976. (Chapters 1, 2, 3, 5, 7, 8, and 9.)

Miller, Gary, and K.M. "Scotty" Mitchell. *Price Guide to Collectible Kitchen Appliances.* Radnor, Pa.: Wallace-

Homestead Book Company, 1991. (Chapter 2.)

Raycraft, Don, and Carol Raycraft. *American Country Antiques*, tenth ed. Radnor, Pa.: Wallace-Homestead Book Company, 1991. (Chapters 1, 2, 3, 5, 7, 8, and 9.)

———. *Collectors Guide to Country Furniture.* Paducah, Ky.: Collector Books, 1984. (Chapters 2 and 6.)

Revi, Albert Christian. *The Spinning Wheel's Complete Book of Antiques.* New York: Grosset and Dunlap, 1977. (Chapters 1, 3, 5, 7, 8, and 9.)

Rinker, Harry L. *Warman's Americana and Collectibles*, fourth ed. Radnor, Pa.: Wallace-Homestead Book Company, 1990. (Chapters 1, 2, 3, 4, 5, 7, 8, and 9.)

———. *Warman's Antiques and Their Prices.* Radnor, Pa.: Wallace-Homestead Book Company, 1991. (Chapters 1, 4, 5, 7, and 8.)

Smith, Carter. *Country Antiques and Collectibles.* Birmingham, Ala.: Oxmoor House, Inc., 1981. (Chapters 1, 3, 5, 7, 8, and 9.)

Smith, Wayne. *Ice Cream Dippers.* Wayne Smith, Walkersville, Maryland, 1986. (Chapter 5.)

Swedberg, Robert, and Harriett Swedberg. *Vintage Advertising Series, Tins 'n Bins.* Radnor, Pa.: Wallace-Homestead Book Company, 1985. (Chapter 1.)

Thompson, Frances. *Antiques from the Country Kitchen.* Radnor, Pa.: Wallace-Homestead Book Company, 1985. (Chapters 1, 2, 3, 5, 6, 7, 8, and 9.)

Time-Life Books. *American Country* series. Alexandria, Va.: Time-Life Books Inc., 1988. (Chapters 2, 3, 5, 7, and 9.)

———. *The Encyclopedia of Collectibles.* Alexandria, Va.: Time-Life Books, Inc., 1978. (Chapters 1, 2, 3, 4, 5, 7, 8, and 9.)

———. *The Life History of the United States.* New York: Time Inc., 1964. (Introduction.)

Vogelzang, Vernagene, and Evelyn Welch. *Graniteware Collector's Guide with Prices.* Radnor, Pa.: Wallace-Homestead Book Company, 1981. (Chapter 3.)

———. *Graniteware Collector's Guide with Prices*, vol. 2. Radnor, Pa.: Wallace-Homestead Book Company, 1986. (Chapter 3.)

Whitmyer, Margaret, and Kenn Whitmyer. *The Collector's Encyclopedia of Hall China.* Paducah, Ky.: Collector Books, 1989. (Chapter 4.)

Catalogs and Periodicals

Montgomery Ward and Company, *Groceries Price List No. 526.* Chicago Avenue Bridge, Chicago, Ill. November and December 1910. (Chapters 1, 3, 5, 8, and 9.)

———. *Spring and Summer 1924 Catalog, no. 100.* Kansas City. (Chapters 1, 3, 5, and 8.)

———. *Summer Sale Catalog 1918.* Chicago, Ill. (Chapters 1, 3, 5, and 8.)

Sears Roebuck and Company. *Fall 1900 Catalog, no. 100* (reproduction). Northfield, Ill.: Digest Book, Inc., 1970. (Chapters 1 and 5.)

The American Home Magazine. 1938 issue. (Introduction; Chapters 2, 3, 5, 6, and 8.)

Woman's Home Companion. 1939 issues. (Introduction; Chapters 2, 3, 5, and 8.)

The Delineator. 1925 issues. (Introduction and Chapter 6.)

Ladies' Home Journal. 1919, 1920, and 1925 issues. (Chapters 2, 3, 5, 6, and 8.)

Articles

Bassitt, Dave, and Randy Bassitt with Marcie Leitzke. "The Red Wing Crockery Craze." *Country Living* (May 1985). (Chapter 7.)

Bloemendaal, Sharon. "Washboards—A Sculptural Folk Art." *The New York-Pennsylvania Collector* (November 1990). (Chapter 5.)

Boyd, Bill. "Salem Witch Spoon Helped Launch Souvenir Spoon Collecting in U.S." *Antique Week* (March 19, 1990). (Chapter 1.)

Carlisle, Lillian Baker. "Souvenir Spoons." *Yankee Magazine* (October 1975). (Chapter 1.)

Ellett, William. "In Search of Vermont Stoneware." *Yankee Magazine* (May 1979). (Chapter 7.)

Gage, Marjorie. "Advertising Memorabilia." *Country Living* (March 1987). (Chapter 1.)

Greco, Gail. "Colorful Kitchen Collectibles." *Country Living* (October 1987). (Chapter 5.)

Griffiths, Marjorie. "Pewter Ice-Cream Molds." *Country Living* (August 1985). (Chapter 5.)

Hazelcorn, Howard, and Jane Hazelcorn. "Collecting Early Electric Toasters: They're Getting Hot." *Antique Week* (January 23, 1989). (Chapter 2.)

Hirsch, Mary. "Festive Fiestaware." *Country Home* (October 1988). (Chapter 4.)

Lux, Heidi. "Morganville's Fragile Redware Has Real Personality." *The New York-Pennsylvania Collector* (November 1990). (Chapter 7.)

Mellish, Susan L. "Yellowware Banded Mixing Bowls Are Favorite Finds." *The New York-Pennsylvania Collector* (November 1990). (Chapter 7.)

Plante, Ellen M. "Antique Ice Boxes." *The New York-Pennsylvania Collector* (March 1989). (Chapter 2.)

―――. "Every Woman's Helpmate: The Free-Standing Kitchen Cabinet." *Country Traditional Decorating Ideas* (Fall 1990). (Introduction and Chapter 6.)

―――. "Hoosier Kitchen Cabinets: A Remarkable Stride in Domestic Engineering." *The New York-Pennsylvania Collector* (October 1988). (Introduction and Chapter 6.)

―――. "In Pursuit of the Hoosier." *Country Living* (April 1988). (Chapter 9.)

Rivera, Betty. "Treenware." *Country Living* (May 1987). (Chapter 9.)

Schneider, Mike. "Fiesta: A Rainbow at the Table." *Antiques and Collecting Hobbies* (August 1988). (Chapter 4.)

Shaw, Dottie M. "Fiesta." *Country Living* (October 1983). (Chapter 4.)

―――. "Old Time Kitchen Tools." *Country Living* (July 1986). (Chapters 5 and 9.)

Stark, Ralph W. "The Boone Cabinet Makers." *Boone Magazine* (March 1977). (Chapter 6.)

Weiss, Gloria K. "Graniteware." *Country Living* (November 1986). (Chapter 3.)

Whorf, Amy. "Carnival Glass." *Country Living* (October 1987). (Chapter 4.)

Index